AS ONE STAGE DOOR CLOSES

The story of John Wade: Jobbing Conjuror

ISBN 1 898576 30 0
First edition

Third Age Press Ltd, 2002
Third Age Press, 6 Parkside Gardens
London SW19 5EY
Managing Editor Dianne Norton

Backcover photo: L to R:
Eric Midwinter, Robin Mackervoy, John Wade

Cover design by Robin Mackervoy
Layout design by Dianne Norton
Printed and bound in Great Britain
by Intype London

AS ONE STAGE DOOR CLOSES

The story of John Wade: Jobbing Conjuror

Eric Midwinter

Contents

Foreword

JOHN WADE: JOBBING CONJUROR

Here's a question for you. What do the following have in common? Windsor Castle; Hamley's toyshop; Peter Sellers; crippling arthritis; *the Avengers*; Pinner; Joan Collins; RAF Wyton; *the Queen Elizabeth*; Tonypandy; Richmal Crompton; the Kray brothers; Billy Graham . . .

There is nothing up our sleeves: those variegated items are simply some of the tasty ingredients that compose the recipe for the life of John Wade, master magician and entertainer.

The guests have dined and wined. They sit back satisfied, but now in expectant mood, for it is cabaret time. Everybody loves a conjuror. Everybody enjoys the benignant outrage of mystification. Everybody delights in the fact that nothing could be more harmless than colourful illusion. The magician has but one purpose – the creation of baffled amusement. Would that everyone – in a world of terror, greed, chaos, suffering and misery – had that same aim in life. It is a wholesome profession and no one has more effectively conveyed that sense of well-being than John Wade.

He steps forward, smartly attired in dinner jacket or lounge suit, according to the occasion. All eyes focus. Yes, he is over 70 now, and, true enough, he may have left his walking stick by his chair. It is equally true that his hair is not so reddish nor so full as in years past, but the lineaments of a strikingly handsome countenance inescapably remain. Of no more than medium height, his presence is still swiftly imposing. The guests, possibly only half-consciously, are beguiled by the sparkling eyes and infectious grin. Neither age can wither nor custom stale those remarkable features. These are the bright eyes and bushy-tailed beam of the schoolboy who believed in himself when others lacked the faith and who won through to international magicianly recognition, hailed by the public and, very importantly, lauded by his peers.

We are at ease in his company. Of course, he might cajole or dupe one or two of us into assisting him in his benevolent deceits, but it is all so unconstrained that no one is at all threatened by this chirpy boy-man. For the moment the agony of a severely damaged spine and the ache of badly stiffened fingers are forgotten, or, more truthfully, the pain is put on hold for our especial benefit, so that we might only see the debonair outline of a convincing performer. Off we go, then, with thimbles appearing and disappearing in eye-boggling confusion; with mirrors vanishing into the black and white hole of today's newspaper; only to experience a perplexing restoration a moment later, with resplendently-hued playing cards dextrously forming and re-forming in luscious array.

The tricks reveal an uncanny technical expertise, but that is barely half the explanation of John Wade's almost casual grasp of the seated guests' attention. Much more is it about the presentation. Undeniably, the insouciance of his approach links in with the trickery, for we are constantly distracted by the effortless conversation. We are listening to the disarming phrases when we should be concentrating on the devious fingers. The lines are pleasantly amusing. These are not for belly-laughs which, in turn, might detain us too long and stop us enjoying the tricks: these witty remarks are rather to keep us deliciously preoccupied. It is not overdone – John Wade is never prolix nor garrulous. It is judged aright, sufficient unto the illusion is the wordage thereof – and, incidentally, sovereign evidence of why John has been in constant demand during his career for compering duties. The humour is gentle and matey. The nearest to a political barb might be 'Mrs Thatcher's done a lot to create more small businesses; mind you, they were big businesses when they started.' There is no malice nor, indeed, any hint of a presumptuous cleverness. This is not a smart-alec or clever-clogs at work. John Wade (if that same Mrs Thatcher will forgive the borrowed coinage) is 'one of us'.

The comfort, the familiarity, of sharing the values of our cabaret artist are so very reassuring. Other acts may stake their all on establishing a god-like separateness. Not John Wade. He appears to be saying; 'look, I'm just a lad who learned these odd tricks; you seem a decent lot; I'd like to share them with you and just chat about them as we go.' Naturally, he is extremely confident and we appreciate that, for, if he were nervous, we would be embarrassed and uneasy. But it is confidence without that brassy sort of arrogance that affronts and disturbs. John Wade is sometimes impertinent about his audience, but, again, it is a mild insolence that never lapses into the abusive or the offensive. He never, for instance, as some comedians do, isolates someone and makes him or her a butt for the rest of the group. The demeanour is as magical as the actual illusions; the presentation as wizard-like as the prestidigitation.

He chatters on, reaching into his jacket pocket for a sealed pack of cards and entrusting them to one of the guests for secure keeping. He puts his hand in his pocket again and this time pulls out a nonexistent pack. He tosses it nonchalantly to another of the guests who, absurdly, pretends to catch it. John then, to much merriment, leads this pressed henchman through the bizarre charade of

Quintessentially John . . . the John Wade *persona* most effectively captured by the gifted Savage Club artist, John Worsley

opening the pack ('don't forget to take the seal off first'), removing the cards, shuffling them, ('I think you've dropped one') and then selecting a card. The bemused helper is invited to show the card to a neighbour, who automatically peers at the empty space ('you're as mad as he is, staring at a card that isn't there'). He must declare what this phantom pasteboard represents and, haltingly, the assistant decides on a card, say, the eight of hearts. Now the charade is reversed. The invisible card is replaced in the invisible deck; the invisible deck is returned to the invisible pack and the invisible pack is thrown back to John Wade who catches it neatly and sticks it back in his pocket. Our attention is now turned to our colleague who has been clinging grimly to the real pack. He is asked to open the real pack and pull out the real cards. Just one real card is facing the wrong way, standing out like a diamond sparkling amidst coal-dust. Except that this diamond is the eight of hearts.

Around the function room one may hear the whispered *cliché* of wonderment: ‘how did he do that?’ It is an exercise in the dialectic of the metaphysical and material worlds. It is as deft a piece of professional conjuring as you are likely to see. Beyond that, moreover, we are bidden, and feign would we deny the chance, to join John Wade in his Puck-like mood of glee and mischief, just as we might relish the animated gaiety of the lively, ever so slightly precocious schoolboy.

Puer aeternus: the classical concept of perennial boyhood . . . John Wade’s genius lies in having preserved some aspect of this precious gift for his adult livelihood and, happily, for some of his larger life. It is not the whole of the picture by any means. John Wade is mature, indeed, seriously so, in many aspects of his character and thought, but, particularly in performance and in company, he has nurtured a degree of ‘eternal adolescence’ that is endearingly captivating.

This, therefore, is John Wade’s story. It is the tale of the adaptability of show-business seen through the eyes of one of its most resilient and talented exponents. In his war-time school days John Wade became a magician. Now in his seventies, he is still a magician; in many ways, still the same magician. In the intervening five or six decades, he has prospered and survived, despite the vicissitudes of his precarious trade. Moving from ‘semi-pro’ to full-time professional in 1953, he has been involved in every possible facet of entertainment, from end of pier to end of

Windmill, from casinos to cruises, from radio to royalty, from Holyhead to Hollywood. His has been a magical career, replete, in his private as well as in his professional life, with wearisome downfalls as well as glorious upturns.

In itself it is a fascinating show-business saga, full of insights into the benefits and disbenefits of a lifelong career in the entertainment industry. But there is an additional dimension. Such is the vast spread of John Wade's experience that his life-story amounts to a personal portrait of how the entertainment business has changed over the last half century, in response, sometimes in gallant, even desperate response, to shifts in the social and economic fabric.

Thus this is a 'bio-documentary'. Not only had John Wade to battle his way from the sober-sided, disapproving environs of 1930s suburbia to the sumptuous glamour of international acclaim, he has also had to duck and dive to adapt his glittering performance to the sudden switches in cultural taste – whilst, all the time, like an ordinary mortal, having to deal with private problems of health and family. Through the lens of this wealth of experience, therefore, we are enabled to watch the extraordinary unfolding of 50 years of the vital history of popular entertainment.

At the end, however, the spotlight really turns on John Wade, irresistibly cheerful, optimistic and forward-looking, that upbeat core of his genuine personality revealed in every flourish of the chameleon-like cards and each twist of the multiplying thimbles, and in every glistening of the twinkling eyes and in each shimmer of the boyish grin. Time now to trace that long, busy lifeline. Time now to answer the question posed by Puck in *Midsummer-Night's Dream*: 'How now, spirit! whither wander you?'

Chapter One
THE 1940s
NEW DOG ~ NEW TRICKS

From whence do magicians come? They used to say that if you wanted a fast bowler in Nottinghamshire (or an inside-right for Newcastle United) all you had to do was whistle at the local pit-head and one would ascend, eyes gleaming white in sooty face, up the mineshaft. Cornet players, all shimmering tremulous scales, were, according to such legends, available at your nearest textile mill, while every Welsh Baptist chapel could provide a tenor or two of soaring resonance. But where do magicians come from? One's half-hope would be that their source would be exotic and mystical. If not the cavern in the mysterious wood, suffused with sulphurous fumes and with the eerie silence broken only by the unnerving chant of incantations over the bubbling cauldron, then surely might one expect, at very least, the eccentric household, bizarre and higgledy-piggledy, replete with astrological charts and Tarot cards.

Of course, reality, dull, benumbing reality, usually contrives to do the tediously unexpected and disappoint. John Wade, who has pursued an astute trajectory through over 50 years of active magicianship, came from a background that scarcely offers a clue as to why he should have joined and adorned the elusive world of magic. He was reared in the Eastcote suburb to the northeast of London. Elongated strings of two-and-a-bit bedroomed semi-detached villas, each with its decent patch of garden, threaded and twisted there. With planning at a discount and with builders using pattern-books rather than fresh-minded architects, the tendency was to follow the lines of existing country roads, rather than to create, for example, quadrilaterals of housing. There was little that was modernist in design. Attempts, much scoffed at by the self-appointed arbiters of taste and the culture-snobs, were made to suggest a mock-Georgian or Tudorbethan effect. Amenities were sometimes slow to arrive. In Eastcote, for example, one had to struggle along a cinder track to the railway station.

It was a sudden movement. Ribbon development proceeded with unusual alacrity. Some three million private houses were erected between the two world wars, often following the lines of transport. Eastcote was part of John Betjeman's *Metroland.* Along with those of Wembley Park, Pinner, Ricksmanworth, Chorley Wood, Hillingdon and Ruislip, its inhabitants obeyed the behest of the Metropolitan Railway Company to migrate thither. Increasingly it was for owner-occupation, but with a resistance, social perhaps more than economic, favouring rental. In effect, the mortgage repayment and the rent were, in a low-price economy, much the same – probably something like 8s or 10s (40p/50p) a week – but some felt vaguely uncertain about the risky imprudence of the mortgage debt.

The story of middle-class life is a saga of cyclic outward expansion from the main urban centres. Where the Pooters of George Grossmith's droll fashion, *The Diary of a Nobody* had resided in the Laurels, Brickfields Terrace, Holloway in the 1880s and 1890s, their social descendants were settling further out in Eastcote, and in a thousand other filaments of semi-detached homes, in the 1920s and 1930s.

Home base . . . the Wade family house in Eastcote, London, as it is today – there was no car and no garage in John's boyhood

George and Amy Wade were children of those 1890s. They had lived in Billericay in Essex, but they had joined their fellow clerks, local government officers, elementary schoolteachers and other white-collared professionals in the march on Eastcote. George Wade, having served in the first world war, in which a nasty inhalation of gas had left him plagued with a lifelong rasping cough, had struggled with the necessary examinations to qualify for the clerical grade of the civil service. Officialdom proffered new chances to the lower middle classes, alongside similarly new opportunities in technical jobs like draughtsmanship and engineering. About this time roughly a fifth of the population were deemed middle class, that is, approximately nine million of the populace. Approaching ten per cent of the occupied population were, in fact, clerical workers: it was a growth industry. Their annual income might have been as low as £200 or £250, although many, of course, did better than that. As a rule-of-thumb, 60% of all those working in the 1930s earned between £125 and £250 a year, with a further 20% receiving between £250 and £500.

George Wade found his clerical *niche* in the supply section of the Air Ministry, whence he daily commuted. Amy Wade stayed at home and kept house, for, unlike the Pooters, there was no servant. Servants were a dying breed, their role as status symbols replaced in the inter-wars years by other marks, such as car ownership. Only 5% of households had a servant in 1931, a dramatic decline from the pre-1914 years. Until war came in 1939, being a housewife was the respectable thing to be, although, when war came, she chose employment in the prim haven of a local solicitor's office. In any event, there was little John Wade to care for. He was a latecomer and, like many latecomers in adult life as in pregnancy, he was a troublemaker, in that he created such problems at birth that the full panoply of Bart's Hospital had to be recruited to ensure his safe arrival on 9 December 1930.

His parents were relatively old when he did finally put in this belated appearance and he was an only child. This is unremarkable. One of the attendant characteristics of the rise of suburbia was the fall of the birthrate. It was already declining across the social echelons, but the drastic fall among the clerical classes amounted to a collapse. Contemporaries noted the absence of children from the long suburban roads and avenues. George Orwell, a graphic critic of the suburban phenomenon, spoke of the middle classes locked in 'the deep, deep sleep of England', by which he meant a social and emotional as well as a physical silence. More raunchily, A J P Taylor reminded us that anyone studying the England of these times had to take into consideration what amounted to an epidemic of sexual frustration.

J B Priestley, in his famous *English Journey*, identified the survival of the rural and the continuance of the working class cultures, but emphasised the third growing cult of suburbia. It was the portent of things to come, of how, in general, the British would conceive of their aspirations, private, restrained and – hence the avoidance of expensive babies – marked by certain materialist standards. As Gracie Fields warbled, 'We've got to keep up with the Joneses.' The church continued to hold some sway among the lower middle classes. Amy and George Wade were regular churchgoers, predictably at the neighbourhood Anglican church of St Lawrence. Affiliation with the state church was of a piece with the upkeep of righteous conduct among these social groups. It was the badge of social conformity rather than a pledge of deeply explored conviction. Thus George and Amy Wade played out, as did thousands of others, a steady, if never wholly intimate, let alone passionate, relationship. Reticence was the admired emblem of the middle-class marriage. A tiny rising spiral of George drinking and Amy being prudishly dismayed was perhaps the sole flaw in the even tenor of the marriage, with the lack of moderation of the one and the lack of forbearance of the other raising the temperature of the ongoing spat.

John Wade's memory was kick-started by the second world war, that forger of many of his generation's remembrances. Beforehand is largely a closed book. Even his first holiday recollection is of the beach at Paignton, five days after the great Robb Wilton festival, 'the day war broke out . . .' There is the vestige of a portmanteau Christmas memory of an annual day spent with Aunt Winnie and Uncle Jim, with the adults committed to earnest discussion fore and aft of the king's painfully stuttering broadcast, and with the

Sand castles in the air . . . a young John Wade, already perhaps considering how he will make things disappear . . .

infant John under the table with his toy soldiers, with only Uncle Jim, not an adept at nor a fan of earnest conversation, making any effort to make personal contact. Under the table John doubled up on the old middle-class stricture: he was neither seen nor heard.

Thus John was a war and wireless child, his stream of consciousness beginning with the world of rationing and radio. The Wades' original wireless depended for life on its accumulator, a dead-weight of cube the size of a biscuit tin, which had to be carried to the nearest radio shop for recharging. These were the days of *Monday Night at Eight O'clock,* with its magazine format of Inspector Hornleigh, 'Puzzle Corner', plus its Deliberate Mistake, Syd 'What would you do, chums?' Walker *et al,* and of Leslie Woodgate with his community singing.

Most famous of all was Tommy Handley, starring in ITMA, an acronym coined from a *Daily Express* headline about Adolph Hitler – *It's That Man Again!* There was music from the Palm Court and on Henry Hall's guest-night, but George Wade was either non-musical or saw in light music some simmering evil and he tended to switch off, rather awaiting the advent of *the Brains' Trust*, with C E M Joad, Julian Huxley and Commander Campbell exchanging their characteristic ideas, or other talk-programmes.

George Wade was evacuated with the Air Ministry to Harrogate, leaving his wife and child to face the London blitz, doodlebugs and VII rockets. The Citizen's War often had that kind of sardonic aspect, with the menfolk sometimes in safer billets than the women and children. Amy and John Wade settled to a war-diet of stews, grey bread and what could be manufactured from stray pieces of liver and offal, and, such was his mother's competence in the kitchen, there was no risk of starvation and most of what was offered was edible. The real pressure was more to do with being the man of the house as a pre-teenager and John Wade grew up quickly as a jobbing plumber and electrician, mending the flooding watertank in the loft whilst Amy suffered a bout of mild hysterics in the kitchen. With Amy taking up employment, John became one of the first generation of latchkey children, fending very much for himself in an environment which, while not socially threatening, was, after all, one beset by the perils of total war. That enforced maturity was perhaps to be one key to his future progress.

Then there was school. One of the grimmer ironies of mid-century society was the tale of not so well-to-do genteel families anxiously scrimping the pounds essential to provide their youngsters with a private education that was heartily detested and assessed, almost certainly rightly, to be irrelevant to the real world. After a couple of years at a Ruislip kindergarten and a spell at the King's preparatory school, Harrow, it was off to the Haberdashers' Aske's school for a five year sentence. John Wade hated it. Apart from some clear-cut mathematics teaching and some enthralling yarns in the history lessons, it was purgatory. The system was unblinkingly banal and rigid. It was the sort of school which insisted on giving you a late mark even when enemy bombing had severely affected rail travel.

Despite the insufferable *ennui*, John managed, through the forced labour of homework grudgingly and, frequently, unpunctually negotiated, to attain his School Certificate, with exemption from Matriculation, then the first step, had the convict willingly submitted to an even lengthier punishment, to college entrance. It was not a bad result and not untypical perhaps of lots of youngsters who, while disliking the construct, were sufficiently alert to compromising with a woefully uninspiring service. He played truant with his mind rather than with his feet.

In any event, John Wade was, in the best traditions of scholarship, a voracious reader, as long as the books were of his own choosing from the public library and not selected by an austere school. Ask him what books he read and the instant answer is 'Just William' books; straight off pat, right away without hesitation. Apart from an obeisance to 'Alice', the rest is about what he didn't read, in particular, the do-gooding champions of Ivanhoe and his pious ilk.

Dare one draw the moral from this and suggest that John Wade was enjoying reading his own sacred text? The anti-hero, William Brown, was created in 1917 by Richmal Crompton (R C Lamburn, 1890-1969, much the same life-span and generation as John's parents) and this classics teacher at Bromley High School based him on a truculent young relation. It should be noted that William is a native of the suburbs, with his posh, if bedraggled, school uniform, and not a denizen of the proletarian confines. He is anti-establishment from within the establishment, fractious at the illogical nature of adult authority and keen to challenge it. Basically, he is eager to reform the ills, as he sees them, of this blinkered adult lifestyle: he is a Che Guevara among schoolboy subversives, keen to put matters right rather than to destroy meaninglessly. Significantly, for this analysis, he is the focus for group action, the leader of the Outlaws, viz, Ginger, Henry and Douglas, almost a satirical take on Harry Wharton's 'Famous Five' at Greyfriars, with their effete japes and tame midnight feasts.

In branding John Wade a school-refuser, it is important to realise that, like William, he did not turn his back, as do so many anti-schoolites, on such educational horrors, but tried valorously to construct an alternative boyhood, not only for himself but for his equally downcast mates. To be fair, a large adjunct to this was his participation in the wolf cubs and in the boy scouts, which, with the church choir, provided the substantive amount of his out-of-house leisure. These, obviously, were formalised activities, but, crucially, they were not school-based. Indeed, he became a King's Scout, a firm token to his stickability in areas where his interest was engaged. These pastoral and vocal pastimes were organised in and around St Lawrence's Church, making it very much a family focus. He was – who isn't, to some extent? – anti-parent, but it was not as if he was out thieving and vandalising. The knotty ethical problems of the Wade household revolved around such theological posers as to whether or not it was sinful to take a bike ride on Good Friday.

As for hobbies, he was an enthusiastic stamp-collector and aeroplane modeller, a hobby much expanded with the coming of aerial warfare and an increased motley of planes. But he was not a solitary philatelist nor a modelling isolate. Just as he became a leading light in the scouts and, after some untypical butterflies, a soloist and duetist in the choir, he was a non-formal administrator of stamp-collectors and aeroplane modellers, especially at school. He was not the school refusenik who opts for the lonely patrol of the shopping arcades: this was not escape from but to . . . to the joys of organising others in non-school projects. The notion of the hidden curriculum had not then been invented by serious-minded educational sociologists, but John Wade was already helping to set its syllabus.

As with Henry, Douglas and Ginger to William, the boys, the other stamp and plane buffs, flocked to his standard. He had discovered a flair for people-management. It really is difficult to spot its provenance. Unless an unknown jester perches on a low branch of the Wade family-tree, one may rule out genetic inheritance, if a strait-laced mother and a buttoned-up father are any guide. Existence in an introverted house in an introverted *milieu* in an introverted decade puts the damper on any argument in respect of nurture. From some profound psychological depths, John Wade found the inestimable gift of *camaraderie*. He discovered that he could charm his peers and endear himself to them.

This miniature art-form applied to girls. At a time when many youths, especially only children and those at single-sex schools, found the opposite gender embarrassingly painful to contemplate, John, in this facet the converse of William Brown *apropos* the emetically challenged Violet Elizabeth Bott, was chatting up the pretty young damsels who attended the church socials or were to be tracked down waiting on station platforms *en route* for their own single-sex schools. He was never short of girl- or boyfriends. It has to be said that, at this juncture, this was a social skill that had little or no emotional attachment. John Wade has not a single contact left with any of those boys and girls; indeed, he can barely recollect them by face or by name. (A couple of blokes visited him backstage when he appeared at the Windmill, claiming they were old school acquaintances, but, then, lots of lascivious oglers would claim anything to get backstage at the Windmill.)

It must be urged that this was not at base a happy time for John Wade: the informal stamp and model groups; the scouts and the choir; even the friendly girls, joining him for a cycle ride through leafy lanes: these were all strategies for dealing with a fundamental disenchantment. John could not wait to eschew what he felt to be the shackles of childhood and youth. The post-Carrollian view of the innate childlike-ness of children and the modern opinion that childhood should be treasured in its own right passed him by, as, it must be said, it did – and does – thousands of other children oppressed, not by physical, but by spiritual and social harnessing.

Confidence . . . the hallmark of success in all the extrovert trades and professions. Out of nowhere or, possibly, just as a sheer, direct confrontation with the circumspect bureaucracy of parents and school, John Wade had crafted the first necessary component in the magician's armoury. At a more mundane level, one can spot another skill evolving. John was a busily practical lad. The DIY plumbing; the dexterity with Baden-Powell's intricate knots; the delicately-constructed model planes; the inevitable Meccano; his own bow to this sporting life in that he was a wily slow bowler at cricket – these all add up to an indispensable asset for the conjuror. This ability to build and handle artefacts with assurance was another important attribute.

And yet . . . it is still a giant step for mankind from the dreadful hush of Eastcote to the lavish applause of the Hippodrome audience. What directed this youngster with some sort of inbuilt charisma and a talent for manual adroitness towards the Magic Circle? His was not a family for going out much. He recalls ever so dimly a pre-war pantomime with Jessie Matthews as principal boy and he made the regulation trip of all his generation of juveniles to see the 1937 Walt Disney film of *Snow White and the Seven Dwarfs,* in his case at the New Gallery cinema, Regent's Street. This was a veritable safari to the West End, followed by tea at a Lyon's Corner House, where, apparently, he used his ham sandwich to conduct the string *ensemble* as it 'Hi-hoed' its way through the Snow White gems. That extrovert streak again . . .

Such treats indicate that John Wade's parents were worried but not unloving. This was not a cheerless household. It was one where mother and father were anxious to prepare their son properly for a harsh world, but also one in which, for all the reserve typical of the mid-20th century heartlands of suburban England, there was a desire that John should have a happy life. In particular, George Wade could sometimes relax and enjoy a joke with a son who recalls him with affectionate sentiment. The home was not free of laughter. Their anxiety about John, which would reach something of a peak with his insistence on conjuring as a career, was motivated by a genuine concern for him screened through their own values, not by any negative or scoffing impulse to belitttle or ignore him.

Show-biz seemed a distant prospect. John would start to go locally to the local Eastcote cinema when he was a little older, but, unlike many families of the age, there was no standard weekly visit to the movies nor to the variety theatre. Then once, during the war, George Wade, presumably on a holiday-in-reverse from Harrogate, took John to the Golders Green Hippodrome to see The Great Lyle, a magician who, after one of the patterns of the time, produced the entire show, complete with a flying gramophone. Maybe there was a seed sown there, for, according to the replay tapes of always suspect memory, this was the first sighting by the future wizard of a then present-day member of that arcane species.

Probably The Great Lyle was remembered when, at Christmas 1946, someone – who was this mystery begetter of a splendid career? – gave the 16 year-old John a box of conjuring tricks as a festive gift. He mastered them quickly, apart from a card-exchange device that failed to work. After school, one wintry January evening, he intrepidly made his way to Hamley's in Regent's Street, from where the Christmas box had been purchased, and upbraided the man at the magic counter. Patiently, the assistant demonstrated to John how to make the card change colour. He was Len Allen, who, as Lenz, did a fire-walking act, with which he coupled other discomforting feats, like threading needles through his tongue, but who, in leaner moments, manned the Hamley's conjuring sales point.

He then said the magic words to John. These were not 'Abracadabra', but 'come back next week and show me'. This John, greatly enthused did, and he received his first coaching. Len Allen, who, unconsciously, seems to have had all the virtues of the finest adult educators, ruled out any further purchases of magical materials, which John, allured by colourful silk handkerchiefs, was keen to buy. Len Allen was aware that 1s 6d (just over 7p) weekly pocket money did not stretch to many colourful silk handkerchiefs but, economic judgement apart, he realised that a 3s 6d (just over 17p) conjuror's textbook was worth a laundry-basket-full of coloured silk handkerchiefs. He also introduced John Wade to the author of this book, one Edward Victor, an expert in sleight-of-hand, and, unobtrusively, they monitored the youngster's progress. Back he went home to his Eastcote bedroom to practise *legerdemain,* with playing cards tumbling over the bed, as he sought to control their involuntary motions.

There was another element in this nascent magician's career. On a rare summer holiday, at Clacton, John Wade was engrossed by a children's entertainer, Eric P Wilson, a member of the resort's concert party. Again showing that boldness of social approach, John ingratiated himself with the seaside entertainer and spent much of the holiday with him, helping him with his props and, importantly, noting and admiring the inventive and precise fashion in which he constructed his own gadgets. This was to be another influential relationship. Moreover, armed with the season ticket that conveyed him to and from school, he undertook pilgrimages to the Finsbury Park Empire, the Lewisham Hippodrome or whichever theatre had a magician on the bill, such geniuses as Maskelyne or Dante. The tyro avidly watched them all and, as a useful bonus, he inadvertently watched all the other variety top-liners as well.

The apprentice learned rapidly and was soon ready to take on the public. His first two spots were both critical in different ways. One of them was in the Eastcote scout gang show. John manufactured a stage fire and a washing tub, into which he popped sundry items of laundry; he added washing powder, but, come the twist, he accidentally used shrinking powder, and there was the amusing switch to tiny garments. This went well; there was applause for the first time, and there was more. A senior scouter praised him, saying 'you're good at that.' It is sad to relate that the teen-aged John records that as being the first time anyone had ever spoken to him thus positively. Hitherto, at home and at school and perhaps at church, it had all been you mustn't or you couldn't. That cameo is recalled with crystal clarity as a truly regenerative moment and one that set John on the road to magical stardom.

The other show was the school end-of-term concert, with John taking his leave of the school he had, institutionally, loathed. He was determined both to prove he had some talent, even if it were not in the conjugation of irregular French verbs or the recitation of chemical formulae, and also to cock a final and highly theatrical snook at authority. As is recorded with somewhat synthetic calm in the school magazine (John's first review, incidentally), he had a beautiful assistant, in the lissom shape of his current girlfriend, in fishnet stockings, albeit with modest skirt, that the assembled Haberdashers be not convulsed into orgasmic frenzy, and he smoked a cigarette. Actually, he did not smoke and was not even a behind-the-cycle-sheds for devilment smoker. But he smoked a cigarette in the school hall and the authorities had but the cold comfort that he made it vanish. He wore white tie and tails. Whence they came, he knows not or at what cost, although they may have been a waiter's second-hand rig: John cannot remember a time when he did not have white tie and tails. It was a sensational minute or two in the ancient history of that formidable old establishment.

John Wade left school and used the imminent call of national service to defer discussion as to his vocational future and also to scupper any parental hopes of a university placement. To utilise a national service expression, he swanned around for the few months awaiting recruitment. There was something about an interview for employment with a bank, all very vague and misty; there were more cycle rides with more girlfriends; someone gave him an ageing ventriloquial dummy; he began lovingly, like all the great magicians, to assemble his own props; he did some children's parties; and he earned his first fee – of two guineas – performing at a church social.

By now his thunderstruck parents were horrifyingly aware that their aspiration that he might secure what, in the argot of the day and of the lower middle and upper working classes, was 'a safe job' was being thwarted. This now explicit desire to be a conjuror was anti-authoritarianism gone mad. They could see with all too baleful lucidity that this was not a hobby or a phase. They thought he had delusions of grandeur. They felt that going on the stage was precarious and not respectable. He would fail in abject poverty and anyhow it was shaming; it was obscurely anti-church and their attendance at St Lawrence's would be an opprobrious experience. It was long past the point where they would help him with a trick or encourage this vainglorious folly in any way. Perhaps they hoped that the RAF would make a man of him, instil *bourgeois* discipline and direct him onto the straight and narrow path to the nearest bank or council office.

The RAF did the reverse. The RAF, caught, like the rest of the armed services between the demise of the war-time show-business organisation ENSA and the advent of Combined Services Entertainment (CSE) a little later, was bereft of entertainers when it had on its hands thousands of young men who were not the most willing of participants and for whom there was often not a major amount of martial tasks to occupy them. The RAF was more in need of magicians than pilots and, if anything was required to consolidate John Wade's magicianly destiny, it was his 1948 to 1950 service with the air force. Even at Padgate, during induction and basic training, his conjuring skills were artlessly drawn to the attention of officialdom. There was also mention, given his good school and his half-decent school certificate qualification, of a short-term commission, but that meant an extra year and John Wade was still eager to negotiate the institutional duties of childhood and young manhood as swiftly as possible.

He chose instead to do the longest course he could find, a six months wireless operators' programme at RAF Compton Bassett, which raised him to the rank of Leading Aircraftsman. He then spent the remainder of his service at RAF Wyton, close enough to home to scrounge an airlift to Hendon most weekends and remove himself from the claustrophobia of the camp. On each of those stations, and with the encouragement of the powers-that-were, usually after a rollicking display of magicianship in the officers' mess, John Wade started and managed a concert party. He had scarcely been in the RAF five minutes when he was sent home to collect his props and, inevitably, his white tie and tails.

Where most national servicemen were looking to avoid responsibility, the zestful John Wade, at each of these RAF bases, stuck up an invitation on the camp board, welcoming all-comers, the amateur singers, comics and recitationists of, notably, 'Albert and the Lion' or 'the Green Eye of the Little Yellow God'. Twice, then, he formed concert parties, as well as acting as disc jockey for the station radio studio. He devised two-hour shows and, apart from the home base, these were in demand at other RAF installations, military hospitals and the like, to the degree of a couple of shows a week. John Wade was sufficiently self-assured to take a rise out of senior officers in the audiences, employing a couple as blindfolded assistants, for example, hanging the 'fifteen minute interval' sign between them and abandoning them on the stage.

Imagine the insouciance of this enterprise. It is amazing, possibly, for the ordinary mortal, maddening. Here is an inexperienced hand, with a scout gang show, a school concert, a church social and two guineas' income behind him, overseeing, from the lofty height of LAC rank, entertainments for a swathe of RAF personnel. Those who did national service will ruefully recall that 'skiving' – briskly marching through the barracks, for instance, clutching a sheaf of officious-looking documents – was as sophisticated a skill as fan-language in the French *salons* of pre-Revolutionary Paris. On the contrary, John Wade, ebullient to the point of brashness, sought ceaselessly to push himself into the face of the RAF authorities so that he might pursue his chosen trade. One begins to spot the difference (the minor issue of great talent temporarily shelved) between the many who are called to sing in the bath and the few who are chosen to sing at Covent Garden.

Something of that nerveless, mischievous trait was made manifest the day customs officers entered the control tower at RAF Wyton. A flight of bombers was returning from the Middle East, complete, hence the tipped-off excise-men in the operations room, with bomb-bays full of contraband. The customs officers were present to halt any wireless communication to the incoming smugglers, but they had forgotten about Morse. Wireless Operator LAC Wade tapped out a message; the bombers pulled out of their descent and attempted a rerun, which took them low over the camp's married quarters, whereon carpets, containing other items of value, were jettisoned. Sharp-witted, adroit, bold, John Wade was still challenging authority with the cheerful aplomb that would thereafter characterise his show-business *persona.*

Demobilisation from the RAF must have been like the ending of a long theatrical run. The veteran of a hundred shows and a carpet smuggling scam was back in Civvy Street where entertainment was provided courtesy of well-established theatre managements and agencies. John Wade's parents remained opposed to the show-biz dream. When John had wanted to print cards to advertise his availability, his father had forbidden him to use their Eastcote address, whilst, as in most households then, there was no telephone. John might have billed himself as 'the Clandestine Conjuror'.

He was nearly 20 and a living had to be earned. He tried cigarette sales, hawking his wares around the shops. He tried cinema management, living in digs in Hanley as assistant manager of the local Odeon, and then moving to its Uxbridge counterpart. He tried publishing, on the production side, with the Falcon Press, but found the pay virtually nonexistent. As for the magic, he was able, at least, to designate himself a semi-professional, by dint of a show

The Learning Curve . . . John Wade in his first job as an assistant cinema manager – but already performing his magic at the children's matinee

or two a week, a Masonic here, a hot pot supper there. Through the post-war streets, still dingy and woebegone after the neglect and damage of long warfare, he ferried his equipment on bus and tube to archaic Masonic Lodges and chilly social clubs. He never stopped striving. Even as an assistant theatre manager in Hanley, he had done his act at children's Saturday matinees, a feat of some courage, close to foolhardiness, given that those occasions resembled Colin Welland's definition of the school Christmas party: 'Nuremberg with custard.'

Nearly three years had passed, in this unsatisfactory mix of unappealing jobs and inadequate 'semi-pro' dates, when his adventurous grasping of the nettle was illustrated once again. John Wade was passing the Irving Theatre in London's Irving Street and spotted the current show's director taking a breather outside. Knowing him by sight (for, so absorbed in show business was he, he knew everybody by sight) John hailed him breezily. There was a craze for intimate revue at the time; the Globe Revue, the Lyric Revue and, ineluctably, the Irving Revue. They were a combine of the tinselly musical comedy-type revues of the between-wars years and a more adult kind of sub-Cowardesque cabaret. They were smart, thought themselves clever and were a trifle self-indulgent. They made a heady appeal to a Metropolitan audience that wished to feel it had kicked over the moral traces of the pre-war years and was obeying the historian's injunction that the second world war had swept away inhibitions. They were rather knocked on the head a year or so later by the sparse intellectual appeal and sheer wit of *Beyond the Fringe*, when Alan Bennett, Jonathan Miller, Peter Cook and Dudley Moore exquisitely pushed forward and re-defined the boundaries of revue.

John Wade belligerently posed the question of the startled director as to why he had not deployed a magician in his extravaganza. He rallied, extemporising, inquiring what John might be able to contribute to such late-night delights. Cocksure and unfazed, the putative wizard told him exactly what he could contribute – and he was booked. As well as joining in the black-out sketches and other pieces, he did a seven minute conjuring spot. Complying with the daring mood of such theatre, he included a trick which involved the disappearance of a show-girl's bra. Complying with the Lord Chamberlain's implicit wishes, that curvaceous wench wore a duplicate underneath.

Many actors and entertainers yearn long years for a West End booking; many never make it. Composed and persuasive, John Wade actually made his theatrical debut in the West End. The show had a six week run and Rachel Roberts, later to make a name as a film star in such gritty films as *Saturday Night and Sunday Morning* and *This Sporting Life,* and later still, in 1980, to commit suicide, was in the cast. The omniscient Kenneth Tynan reviewed the revue in the London *Evening Standard* and was uncommonly sniffy about the whole business. John Wade came closest to escaping the sting of that incisive pen. He described John as 'the least pretentious act in the show.'

However, it was quite a breakthrough. Above all, it made him visible. And there was a bonus in one of those political accidents that boost or diminish the chances for entertainers. In its way, it is a minute illustration of a central theme of this study; namely, the changes in the social fabric, for better or for worse, that affect the opportunities for show-business people. 1953 was Coronation Year. Suddenly everyone wanted a magician. There were street parties galore and celebratory dances and dinners by the score. Business boomed. Quite abruptly, the other half of the 'semi-professional' circle began to be filled and John Wade is legitimately able to date his full-time professional status from 1953. He was 22.

Among this thrilling rash of spots to do and parties to entertain came the exciting summons to be a guest-star for a week in a summer show at Westgate-on-sea, some miles from Margate on the Kent coast. It was John Wade's first seaside booking and it went swimmingly. With both a West End and a seaside date inscribed thereon, his, until then, near-virginal CV looked healthier. Gloriously, he was booked for variety, still the bread-and-butter for the profession. John Wade had wrestled mightily with the wet blankets of drab conformity, with the negative hosts of gentility, and with those forces of tedious reason and safe jobs, for whom colour and light and, unforgivably, laughter, were judged as questionably suspect. Just William was the Conqueror.

It was next stop the Tonypandy Empire.

Chapter Two
THE 1950s
THE PATTER OF MAGIC FEATS

Tonypandy then was a conclave of colliers encircled by sheep. The Industrial Revolution had thrown up some bizarre dichotomies of pastoral beauty and grimy beast, like the grim shipbuilding gantries overlooking bounteously flowing rivers and tumultuous seas, or the smoky woollen mills set hard by the broad streams of the verdant Yorkshire dales. Since the 1840s a swathe of rich coalseams, some 45 miles in length, had been exploited across South Wales and the mine shafts had risen, gaunt and black, out of the deep valleys. Tonypandy stood in the awesomely impressive Rhondda Fawr Valley, some 25 miles northwest of Newport, with mountain sheep as abundant above as were the coalseams below its craggy landscape.

Tonypandy was, according to the 1951 census, a township of 10,691 souls, one of some ten mining communities, each much the same size, in the Valley. It is a mark of the incidence of 'live' theatre in Britain then that so small a town could boast a variety venue. The grand opening of the New Tonypandy Empire occurred on Monday 15 1909 – 'one of the prettiest and most comfortable halls outside London', claimed the proud local press, and one that could offer its capacity of 2000 customers 'great strength, beauty and comfort.' Its sorrowful closing happened when the demolition gangs began their architectural vandalism in January 1964. A Woolworth's store was erected in its stead. In between whiles the citizens of the Rhondda had witnessed plays, such as *The Dumb Man From Manchester* (surely a contradiction in terms) and appearances by well-known acts from Charlie Chaplin to Tommy Trinder. In the twilit post-war years of variety, it succumbed to the lure of somewhat frowsty shows such as *Folies Montmartre,* allegedly adapted from the Famous French 'Latin Quarter' and, given the scant opposition, truthfully hailed as 'the Naughtiest Show in Town.' With its static nude models and not very high class supporting acts, less exact was its prophecy that it was 'the Show of the Future'. *Folies Montmartre* preceded John Wade by seven weeks.

The Empire certainly rang the social changes. Ominously, the theatre had turned to the silver screen at an early age and had shown silent films, so that it had the double honour of displaying Charlie Chaplin in the flesh and on celluloid. Tom Mix and Mary Pickford were also featured in those early times, with *Blackmail,* shown in 1929, both Tonypandy's and Alfred Hitchcock's first 'talkie'. 'Live' theatre was then revived, with the likes of Jessie Matthews and Rene Houston. A few weeks before John Wade's appearance at the Empire, the Young Welsh Theatre Group performed Emlyn Williams' play, *Trespass.* As variety began to fade, there was another round of cinematic entertainment. Later still, films were intermingled with Bingo. By the late 1950s almost a fifth of women from the semi-skilled and unskilled social categories were, not least in Tonypandy, responding to the enticing tocsin of the bingo caller.

At the time John Wade paid his fleeting visit to the Valley, there was one other theatre, the Grand in nearby Pentre, while the

Rhondda had, apart from the intermittent screenings of the Empire, eight other cinemas, two of them in Tonypandy itself. As some enjoyed the salacious improprieties of *Folies Montmartre,* for example, the local Picturedrome offered Danny Kaye in *Wonder Man* and Walt Disney's *Dumbo*, whilst the Plaza was screening Errol Flynn and Maureen O'Hara in *Against All Flags* and Donald O'Connor in *Francis Goes to West Point.* This wealth of theatrical and cinematic entertainment was available in the 23,000 acreage of the Rhonnda urban district council and for its 111,389 residents. The coming cull of theatres and then cinemas was to carve cultural swathes through such areas.

Tonypandy, therefore, was of a size and character of a thousand and more towns that boasted a variety theatre. Some of them had direct theatrical connections. George Formby Senior, 'the Wigan Nightingale', had practically erected that borough's pier single-handedly. Father, of course, to the irrepressible and highly-successful ukulele strummer, the other George Formby, the older man had created a much more complicated *persona* than his son. He was the melancholy, diffident type who genuinely believed himself to be light-hearted and outgoing. That approach – the introvert with an extrovert complex – was an astonishingly difficult posture for the music hall stage. Only Tony Hancock, in modern times, has even hinted at such a configuration, but so completely did the elder George Formby preserve this countenance that he was one of only two acts – Dan Leno was the other – that Marie Lloyd would deign to watch. In her turn, Gracie Fields, having been born over a fish and chip shop within its bailiwick, brought a similar dubious fame to Rochdale, describing, for instance, in one of her songs the rum events that befell those who joined her in 'Following the Rochdale Hounds.'

Tonypandy was not a 'comedian's town' in this respect, but its name was synonymous with a chapter in the bleak saga of British working class history, rather like Jarrow, 'the town that was murdered', with its renowned unemployment march in the 1930s. Amid a spread of bitter industrial disputes at that time, some 25,000 miners, employed by the hard-headed Cambrian Coal Trust in the Rhondda and Aberdare Valleys, went on strike in 1910. The Tonypandy pithead was attacked by local miners and the ventilating machinery damaged. There were three days of rioting and sacking of a motivation and on a scale dependent on whether one reads a right-wing or a left-wing account, and police drafted in from Bristol and Swansea seemed unable to cope. Winston Churchill was then Home Secretary in Asquith's Liberal administration and that pugnacious politician responded to the Glamorgan Chief Constable's request for troops by mustering 200 hussars and two companies of infantry. Although he cautiously delayed them at Swindon and pleaded for calm, they had to continue their journey, together with a mounted body of Metropolitan policemen. The troubles ended without, thankfully, loss of life, apart from one man killed accidentally in a scuffle, but, thereafter, Churchill, for all his derring-do in the second world war, was vilified in those areas allegedly for confronting the miners with troops.

Tonypandy, then, stood proxy for hundreds of like communities and its Empire Theatre had its many parallels in the Rochdale Hippodrome, the Wigan Hippodrome or the Jarrow Palace. And, on Sunday 7 June 1953, just days after the Coronation, John Wade, unsuspecting of these tales of militant class-conflict, made the railway trip to Tonypandy, humping his luggage with him. You can still take the train to Tonypandy: change at Cardiff and then chug up the Valley from Cardiff Queen's Street Station, through Llandaf and Pontypridd, which is five miles southeast of Tonypandy, on the route to Treherbert. The first objective was to find accommodation. Some theatres were open on Sunday evenings for the receipt of hampers and some kept lists of local landladies; otherwise the police station was the best bet for suggestions about lodgings. Accommodation was, with much relief and without undue worries about its attendant comforts, discovered.

Monday morning, ten o'clock, was band-call. The artists paraded. They placed their music parts on the stage and, first come, first served, took it in turns to rehearse with the pit orchestra. Luckily, the top of the bill often opted to go last so that he or she could take time over ensuring all was well. In such a theatre the band was composed of a dozen semi-professional musicians, who doubled up with a spot of window-cleaning or an insurance collection round. They were paid just two or three pounds for the privilege of playing on and off the likes of John Wade.

Problem number one for John. He had no music. He placed a blank piece of paper on the stage and found that *rara avis*, a sympathetic musical director or MD. Informed that John's act was of gently cheerful bent, he recommended *Whispering* for 'on' and 'off' music, which was all that was required, save for an occasional clash of the cymbal or thwack of the base drum to signal the completion of yet another astonishing piece of magic. He undertook to plot, for a modest consideration, some band parts, so that the young conjuror would have them available for future bookings. *Whispering* it was and remained for some time, until John Wade changed to the more frolicsome *If my friends could see me now*, made famous by the feisty Shirley MacLaine in the screen adaptation of *Sweet Charity* in 1969. The theatre paid a music license and, each week, the MD forwarded a return of what music had been used to the Performing Rights Society so that crumbs of royalties might be sent to the copyright holders, rather like the present-day system where pennies are accumulated by authors from public library loans or photocopyings.

Thus to problem number two. John Wade had no lighting plot and he needed some spotlights or whatever to enhance the act. Forward came an equally sympathetic stage electrician, who quickly drew up a lighting plot for John, again, for some inconsiderable recompense, an investment, for, like the musical 'dots', he could produce it, with a professional flourish, at successive venues.

First of the many . . . John Wade's first professional publicity still

Problem three had been foreseen. The front-of-house manager approached, inquiring after photographic stills for the theatre foyer and windows. John Wade had had fetching likenesses made and framed and they were soon adorning the vestibule. He learned the rule that the good pro always keeps his stills, lighting chart and band parts at the top of his skip for convenient dispatch.

Problem four was easily resolved. With but a tiny troupe of entertainers, even such a second-tier hall as the Tonypandy Empire could manage a dressing-room apiece. Off went John Wade to his, to create, like a legion of performers before and since, out of a foreign corner some semblance of home, with the tablecloth, the makeup (another personal cost), the personal *bric-à-brac*, later the kettle, later still, the consoling bottle. It had been a busy morning. Then it was time for a stroll round the town, back to the digs for refreshment, and a return walk to the theatre for the two evening shows.

There could not be a more overtly honest descriptor than 'variety'. Take that 1953 Tonypandy Empire bill by way of explication. There were just seven acts, each doing a ten minute spot, two of them offering a contribution in each half, and with the bill-topper having a longer spell at the end. Top of the bill this week was Marcia Owen, 'Radio's Personality Singer', with Albert Sadler (almost a famous name) at the piano. Film, records and radio underpinned variety, even as they also undermined it. They made the public aware of entertainers, but they also persuaded the public to take their leisure elsewhere. Marcia Owen was to be heard on popular radio programmes, like *Variety Bandbox* on a Sunday evening, with upthrusting stars like Frankie Howerd, and her Welsh credentials probably carried some resonance in the tuneful valleys and the land of song.

The others all had their own bill-matter as to the manner born. The Darrella Sisters, 'Dancers Supreme', opened each half, and they were variously succeeded by Sadie Corre, 'the Mighty Atom', Freddie Carlisle, 'Comedy Vocal Impressions', Marie Syrett and Pauline Cecil, 'Laughter in a Big Way' and Chris Wortman, 'It's All Madam', to say nothing of John Wade, 'Magically Yours'. Sometimes such bills were only thrown together at the last minute, with local printers themselves showing magical accomplishment in producing posters and programmes on schedule.

Variety grew out of the old-time music hall, although the one had been as formally structured as the other was, by contrast, riotously undisciplined. Music hall had chiefly consisted of singers in character rendering songs, together with audience participation, that were normally their sole prerogative, like Marie Lloyd naughtily relishing the fact that *A Little of What You Fancy Does You Good.* Sometimes these were interspersed with speciality acts, often with a circus ambience, such as jugglers or acrobats, but the singer/song formula was rigorously standard. There were indeed occasional magicians, and the famed ones, like Chung Ling Soo or Houdini, would promote their own shows or top the bills of others, whilst the lesser breeds of magician were more likely, a century ago, to have been fire-eating or sword-swallowing on the travelling fairgrounds.

From about the end of the First World War variety superseded music hall and, in a word, it was nothing but speciality acts, from thought-readers to sea-lions. It was about this same time that the term 'comedian' began to be applied to joke-tellers, perhaps emerging from the George Robey tradition. Hitherto a comedian had been a comic actor, the obverse of tragedian or tragic actor. Now they were gagsters, usually finishing with a song, rather than interrupting a mainline number with some oral commentary, like Gus Elen or George Formby Senior had done. Some magicians assimilated elements of this jokery into their acts, as opposed to the strong, silent types, all flowing tails, sinuous movements and fluttering doves. In a Royal Command Performance Eric Morecambe, with Ernie Wise as Gloria, his glamorous assistant, was to burlesque this convention, with his leaking feathers and his urgent whisper down his sleeve of 'send the budgie up.'

John Wade, playing off the strength of his intrinsically engaging personality, was one of the talkative not the mute brigade, the chatter at once being part of the essential distraction, that chief weapon in the wizard's armoury, and an actual attempt to achieve friendly terms with the audience. At this juncture his act included the multiplying thimbles, the luxuriously fanned playing cards, the floating ball, the revolving candlestick and the vanishing mirror, all processed with a pleasing line in deprecating, conversational humour. It was the buttonholing technique of the chap in the saloon bar or waiting for a haircut at the barber's: nothing ornate, nothing outrageous, just a genial, sociable pitch. It was with some accuracy that he shortly coined his own punning bill-matter, 'the Patter of Magic Feats.'

John Wade rarely had the stage set with sumptuously be-clothed table bearing bottles, boxes and other impedimenta. As here at Tonypandy, his number would shine out on each side of the proscenium arch and, to the lilt of *Whispering*, he would stroll on stage and deploy his topper as container and his gent's cane as its tripod. Wise beyond his youthful years, he did this for three reasons. First, variety was awash with magicians. John Wade preferred the audience to greet him as an entertainer, with part of the mystery being what brand of performer he would turn out to be. The static table, laden with sorcerer's goodies, was a give away. Second, for an audience perhaps *blasé* about the stream of conjurors that swept by them, there was, he reasoned, a temptation to watch the table rather than its owner, counting off the items and inwardly groaning because there was still the bowl of goldfish to be 'vanished'. Third, his approach was a Godsend to stage managements, never an imprudent step to take. Apart from reducing their labours, it meant that John need rarely stray beyond the 'number ones', in theatrical *patois*, the sector between the house curtains or tabs and the first stage tabs. John Wade would commonly 'work in ones' and certainly 'finish in ones'. Gradually, he was mastering the internal sciences of the variety theatre.

So the week progressed. There was the usual goodish house on Monday, when the holders of free tickets, the landladies where the artists stayed and the butchers, bakers and candlestick makers whose shops bore the posted news that the Darrella Sisters *et al.* were in town, received their just deserts. The weekday houses were mixed but, as ever, Saturday brought a reasonable gathering of miners and their families. The days took on a shape of their own. There was the luxury of the late rising and breakfast at ten; there was a chance to do some shopping or catch a movie (golf was strictly for the high flyers, although local club members would always be proud to boast of an afternoon's round with one of the notables of the stage) before having a high tea in the lodgings about 4.30 pm – and there would be a late supper awaiting after the two houses. The young bachelor opted for full board as being more convenient and less expensive.

The evening at the theatre was subject to as strict a temporal discipline as that of the barracks or the factory. All the artists had to abide by the 'thirty minute rule', that is, they had to be backstage a half hour before the show began – in some theatres signing in, rather like the town halls and government offices of the day. That was, in fact, 5.25 pm, for, like the army, an extra five minute law obtained. 5.25, albeit in the evening, was the equivalent of the *reveille* bugle or the foundry hooter blowing. As the first show began at 6.0 pm, it was a matter of 'five minutes overture and beginners'. In short, the action really commenced at 5.55 pm. Even if one were not appearing until the second half, the rule was strictly applied. At Tonypandy the second house began at 8.10 pm and everyone was on the way home by 10 pm.

Eventually there was the knotty question of payment. Outside of the grandiose circuits of big city theatres and down among the smaller venues like the Tonypandy Empire, anyone – a local garage owner or builder – might persuade the theatre management that he could put in a bill. Such was here the case. One Ernest Ivan had assumed responsibility for fielding a group of entertainers and then contacted a number of booking agencies accordingly. As a result of his fleeting appearances in the Irving Theatre *Rush Hour Revue* and as a guest at the Westgate-on-Sea summer show, John Wade found himself on the lists of several agents, for, as yet, he had not been taken under anyone's sole wing. These agents often foregathered, like Shylock and his fellow-usurers on the Rialto in Venice, and in much the same careful frame of mind, at the ABC Restaurant in London's Leicester Square. There they would make their selections. One endearing habit was to offer, say, five pounds loudly, so that the negotiatee's *amour propre* would not be offended in the presence of his eavesdropping colleagues, while signalling with three fingers close across the waistcoat to indicate the true state of the tender.

One of these booked him for Tonypandy, at the usual commission of ten per cent. During the week, such was the insecurity of the business, there was a *frisson* about the rectitude of Mr Ivan the backer. The top-of-the-bill, Marcia Owen, did telephone the Variety Artists' Federation to ask for a check on his credentials, for there were many tales of unpaid wages, even although the contracts bound the artists to keep their side of the bargain, whatever prevailed. Anyway, it transpired that Ivan was not so terrible and, as the stage superstition goes, 'the ghost walked on Friday' and everyone was paid on the nail.

As a consequence, there was £12 awaiting at the week's end, whereas Marcia Owen would have made and merited perhaps £40. Now given that the junior local government clerk might have earned £9 a week in that era and the probationer primary schoolteacher £11, that might not seem so miserable for, the churlish might calculate, a total of two hours' work overall, but wait . . . His agent would snaffle £1.4s (£1.20p); his lodgings, full board, would cost £3.10s (£3.50p); his railway fare took another £3; his band parts took care of £1.10s (£1.50); his lighting plot cost 10s (50p) and he had already invested in costume, magical paraphernalia, stills and makeup. Moreover, having observed the anxieties over payment, he judges it prudent to subscribe to an annual membership of the VAF, a measure of trade union solidarity of which the NUM members comprising the bulk of his Tonypandy spectators would doubtless have approved. Even the commissionaire, who returned his photographs and lighting chart on the Saturday evening, expected a two bob (10p) tip. It was rather like that panto gag where Buttons asks Baron Hardup for his wages and where, such are the telling intercessions during the payment, Buttons concludes with a deficit. So much for buying, for example, all those smart clothes and cutting a dash in the fashion that show-biz cracks were supposed to contrive. There was nothing left. It was back to London, battling with his hamper, for John Wade, back to the continued hard slog of evening bookings for after-dinner entertainments and the like, that the wolf might be beaten back from the door.

At least, clutching his *Whispering* band-parts, he was to avoid the scam for which one or two London halls, like the Finsbury Park Empire and the Metropolitan, Edgeware Road, were notorious. The leader of the pit orchestra, the MD, often, as in Noel Coward's variety one-acter about the Redpeppers song-and-dance turn, made the average regimental sergeant-major look quite cherubic. The lugubrious Les Dawson used to explain how his mother-in-law had been expelled from the Gestapo for cruelty and a shadow of this caricature fell across many a theatre conductor. The MDs in question would savage the music scores proffered them at band-call on Monday morning, dashing them to the ground in mock-rage and refusing to play from such tawdry and indecipherable rubbish. The artist, mightily chastened, would then be sternly asked if he or she would like some new 'dots' prepared and he or she had little choice but to comply. At some substantial expense, the entertainer would be presented with an extravagantly embossed series of band parts, which looked as if they had been lovingly illuminated by the monks at Lindisfarne. The upside was that, wherever they appeared thereafter, everyone spotted that they had played one or other of the big London theatres.

Yet all this material concern meant little to the ambitious John Wade. Here was a young man, after some years of frustration and struggle, knowing what he wanted to do and getting out there and doing it. The commitment was high. The distractions of wine, women and song were low. He as yet does not drink; there is, initially, no special girl in his life; and the songs are for professional purposes only. In terms of his memories, few, if any, relate to the dingy lodgings, the sparse rations, the patchy houses, the thin wages, and the torturous train journeys. He stares straight through these at the essential truth of his tangible delight in being a pro, being part of the business, having made it. He is, at last, thoroughly enjoying himself and overflowing with enjoyment. There is a massive disparity between the greyness of the civic surrounds and their allied theatrical conditions and his sheer joy at being a professional magician, bringing pleasure to people.

Across five decades there vibrates the vital exuberance of a young performer scarcely believing in what he assesses as a decent mix of his good fortune and his good management. He has escaped the deadening entrapment of the safe nine-to-five job and is larking about on the stage – for money. Even now that feeling of delectation is palpable.

Nor was this an over-sanguine expectation. During the next few years this young magician, in his mid-twenties, did exceptionally and regularly well. It is true that the variety theatres, such as the Tonypandy Empire, they were a-dying, having enjoyed some 30 or 40 years of fitful dominion. The radio and the cinema had been serious rivals. By the beginning of the 1939-1945 war – the only major conflict in which radio was the prime vehicle of communication – almost everyone had access to the 'wireless'. 20 millions listened in to *ITMA* at home, and a further 10 millions overseas; there were, surprisingly, 12 million earnest listeners for *The Brains Trust*, while, with its regular harvest of well in excess of 20 million pairs of ears, Wilfred Pickles' post-war show *Have a Go* was to be the most successful programme in British broadcasting history. The cinemas – like the Picturedrome and Plaza of Tonypandy and 'Dai Doots', as the cinema in neighbouring Clydach Vale was fondly known – enjoyed a quarter century of glory, sometimes taking over variety and repertory theatres, as well as building lush new premises. In the 1940s and early 1950s 30 million cinema tickets were sold each week and a third of adults – it was much more for children and teenagers went to their local cinema on a weekly basis.

The hammer-blow was struck by television. The Coronation, which so tidily prefaced John Wade's historic descent onto Tonypandy, was, in the longer term, a cultural rather than a political symbol. It marked the advent not so much of the New Elizabethan Age as of the Televisual Age. Nearly 21 million respectful subjects clustered around five million dimly flickering sets on that rainy day and television became the nation's art-form. Up went the bars and shutters at ever more theatres. A city like Manchester, for instance, that had once boasted a score of music halls and variety theatres was gradually reduced to two main theatres. Now there are less than 500 theatres of any description across the nation. Once London alone had 40 variety theatres. As Bob Hope acutely observed, 'television is the box they buried entertainment in.'

Live theatre survived in its staples, notably those aspects that catered for a family appeal. Foremost among these was the summer show. Apart from that gleeful survivor, the pantomime, it was to enjoy greater longevity than any other sub-species of live light entertainment. Its story was a long one. It was as long as the tale of the seaside resort, dating from mid-19th century, when the notion that the ozone was health-giving coupled with the spread of the railways to bring sudden popularity and riches to hitherto slumbering coastal hamlets. In the 1870s the paternalist railway companies magnanimously gave the first paid week's holiday to its employees. Soon, for instance, the tiny townships of Leyton with Warbreck and North Meols were overwhelmed by what had been an even tinier smidgeon of each – Blackpool and Southport.

The teeming promenade, beach and – that Victorian phallic symbol, matched only by the mill chimney – pier were soon the haunt of entertainers, at first singly, like the Punch and Judy man or the sand-artist, and then in troupes. The Christy Minstrels first appeared in Southport in 1860 and the black-face minstrel groups were soon in evidence all around the coast. They were swept aside by the tide of Pierrots in the 1890s, with Clifford Essex forming his party in 1891, with introductory appearances at Bray, near Dublin, and Cowes. Edwin Adeler and Will Catlin were soon to dominate the pierrot scene and before long women pierrots were included, while there was often a change of costume from the traditional frenchified ruffs and bobbles to, for instance, straw cadies and blazers. By the 1914-1918 war the pierrots were transmuting into concert parties, frequently with an inland as well as a coastal incidence, as so captivatingly pictured in J B Priestley's *The Good Companions*, published in 1929. Soon there were Fol-de-rols – a title apparently first used by George Royle in Scarborough in 1911 – or their ilk in every resort, although the Co-optimists were to gain the highest prestige of any of the concert parties.

Holidaymakers tended to return to the same venue each summer, for, with but a week's vacation, it was too perilous to take the chance of a new experience. Similarly, the concert parties and, eventually, the summer shows, presented this same air of hospitable familiarity. Billie Manders' Quaintesques, for example, played the Rhyl Amphitheatre for 29 unbroken years from 1921, until the death of Billie Manders, one of the earliest of the female impersonators and, just to demonstrate the wheels that spun within show-business wheels, the husband of Will Catlin's daughter, Gladys. 1500 attended his funeral in Rhyl in 1950.

The summer show offered a breezy but tranquil afternoon or evening's entertainment for the discerning holidaymaker. Many, of course, operated *al fresco*. Down the prom, for instance, at Rhyl was Will Parkin's open air theatre, where one might enjoy, in a deck chair, the sea-air and the squawk of the passing seagulls as well as the songs and jokes. As many people preferred to stand around the fencing, perhaps for just a half hour or so, as part of their evening stroll, collections were taken, an important reminder that most seaside shows over the years had relied on this form of revenue. It was still known as 'bottling', from the practice of using a bottle that would take coins but from which it was hard for the collector, had he been so tempted, to remove any. At night the bottle would be ceremoniously broken and the pennies distributed. 'Bottle' is a present-day synonym for courage – could there be a connection?

Many stars made their names at the seaside. A bright instance is that of Arthur Askey, who for eight or nine seasons attracted much cheerful attention at Shanklin, in Powis Pinder's annual display of *Sunshine* – Webster Booth, before his charmingly tuneful partnership with Anne Ziegler, was also in *Sunshine*. It was Arthur Askey's success at Shanklin that led to his starring in radio's *Band Wagon*. It was precisely his kind of effervescent amiability that suited the seaside: 'Hello, playmates' was exactly the right tone of affection, just as the silly quips and the alliterative rhymes about bees and moths struck the apt note for those relaxing after 51 weeks dulling toil in the productivity-driven factories and offices of between-wars Britain. The variety halls were often more abrasive, more steely, reflecting the fact that their clients were snatching just a couple of hours away from those selfsame coalseams and spinning-looms or filing cabinets and typewriters.

John Wade came into his own in this lighter, sunnier atmosphere. Its mellow-humoured mood was ideally fitted to his skills and temperament. A handsomely presentable young man, with a pally grin and a beguiling mien, he offered eye-catching tricks with studied affability. It was just what the summer resort audience, all open-necked shirts, floral frocks and sandals, might have ordered. All was done in a spirit of unassuming good humour, while his cross-generational appeal, delighting youngsters and grandparents as well as the workers and their wives, was a decided plus.

Summer shows prospered in the 1950s. The first fruits of post-war affluence helped. Holidays with pay were now the norm. Upwards of 30 million people took an annual holiday in the United

Kingdom in those years. The motor car, already spelling doom to some collective enterprises, such as many football and cricket matches, in fact assisted this continued migration to the coast, with the train and the *char-à-banc* less favoured than of yore. The two million cars of 1948 jumped to the 6 million of 1960. Yet the flight to Spain was still in its infancy; only by 1960 would holidays abroad touch the ratio of one in six of the vacations taken by Britons. From the seaside showbiz angle, the 1950s managed to enjoy the best traits of the 1940s and the 1960s.

Summer after summer found John Wade in profitable magical employ. In 1954 he was in the *Sunshine Follies*, under Will Hammer's management at the Pavilion, Holland-on-Sea, near Clacton. In 1955 it was again the *Sunshine Follies*, but this summer at the more expansive resort of Torquay. In 1956 John was in *Zip* for the holiday season at Broadstairs on the Kentish coast, midway between Margate and Ramsgate. In 1957 he was in *Gaiety at Eight* at Minehead, a Victorian resort of some 9000 souls on the Bristol Channel. This did wondrously well and won the Outspan Oranges award for best summer entertainment in the 'small' shows category. He was immediately booked for a repeat of *Gaiety at Eight* in 1958, but this time just outside Margate, at Westgate-on-Sea, scene of his early guest appearance five years previously. In 1959 he travelled to Cromer, a pleasant resort, population some 7000, 21 miles north of Norwich, to perform in *Dazzle*.

Concert party work required all-rounders. John Wade had to hoof a bit, sing a bit and act a bit, but, willing and agile and rhythmic and talkative, this was no hardship. The paying customers liked the co-operative enterprise, spotting that the magician who had been a postman in the last sketch was an aged retainer in the next one. It all added to the jollity. King Weather ruled. Hot, arid weeks meant a boycotted pier pavilion. (John welcomed the empty seats: 'I hate crowds', he confided to the meagre attendance.) Pelting rain drove the erstwhile holidaymakers into the theatre. This was

Concerted Effort . . . John Wade and others of the cast of *Gaiety at Eight* which won the 1957 award for best concert party, presented by Leslie Henson. John Wade is far left, next to Leslie Henson.

helpful for the budget, but the audience members were resentful. They were meteorological conscripts. They were compelled to attend and there glumly they sat, raincoats steaming, daring the *Sunshine Follies* to please them. A slight drizzle or sea-fret around early evening was, from the aesthetic stance of the cast, the ideal weather.

It was 16 weeks' marvellous work, usually in reasonably salubrious seaside resort digs, somewhere where one could establish oneself comfortably for four months, in often rather attractive environs, a far cry from the slag-heaps and comfortless digs of Tonypandy. Halfway through the run, the impresario booked John

Wade for the next summer season. That meant another wonderful 16 weeks in the book. Moreover, there were Sunday concerts up and down the coast. With narrowly Sabbatarian bye-laws imposing restrictions on the style of show, an entertainer who could conjure up an act in everyday fashion was a welcome proposition. So John Wade laboured over his follies for six days and on the seventh day he travelled to a nearby coastal resort for a Sunday evening spot.

So full a summer season was tantamount to half a year's work. Furthermore, John Wade was signed up for non-summer runs of *Zip* over lengthy phases of the mid-1950s. This was very much a concert party on wheels, with weekly dates and, as at the seaside, everyone contributing to the collective items and providing his or her speciality spot. Each tour was of several weeks, playing theatres like the Hippodrome, Salford; the Granville, Waltham Green; and the Queen's Theatre, Poplar. It was of that last theatre, its patrons mainly callused-handed dockers, many of Lascar and Chinese extraction, of which Tommy Trinder, faced with a poor attendance, exclaimed, 'they're all at the Polo at Hurlingham.'

The tours organiser was no Vasco da Gama. The journeys criss-crossed the newly nationalised British Railways (its original styling) network in illogical manner, rarely following a rational path. There was one licit reason for this. There were sometimes 'barring clauses' in the contracts that halted the big stars in orbit, should they approach too nearly a town where they would shortly be playing – it was feared that, excited by their proximity, the fans might trespass outside the bounds of their parish. At least, the train tickets were booked and the train compartments reserved, a luxurious improvement on the DIY antics of the solo artist in variety. The hampers were also cared for, arriving safely at band-call each Monday morning in the fresh venue. Lodgings had to be found, but, by and large, it was a more civilised and trouble free lifestyle than variety proper.

With the touring revues, the theatre management and the promotion company cut a deal, perhaps splitting the gross takings 60% to 40%. *Zip's* leading light, the comedian, Jerry Jerome, acted on behalf of Will Hammer, the impresario. It was his thankless task to haggle with each theatre manager about the take, especially at the week's end, before that general post that roused a myriad sleeping railway junctions each Sunday morning as the peripatetic theatricals went on the march.

Jerry Jerome quickly realised that John Wade was, in the time-honoured guardroom register phrase, 'sober and properly dressed'. He could be trusted – and he was trusted to participate in the ancient rite of 'counting the house'. As the curtain rose before expectant rows of onlookers, as the orchestra struck up with the opening chorus and as the *Zip* cast belted out that show-business equivalent of the processional hymn, Jerry Jerome counted the stalls and the magicianly teller tcounted the circle. Rapidly, John learned the skill and it is one he retains. Like the seasoned Canadian lumberjack, who can tell you after one glance at a mass of redwood how many trees are there, John Wade was soon able to offer Jerry Jerome a faithful estimate of the numbers present, the better to equip him for his nightly spat over the figures. 'Quite a few in tonight then' – 'yes, but it's Monday, of course; most of them are on passes' – 'the stalls were packed' – 'yes, but you could have shot a stag in the circle'. . . In such conditions it paid to have adroit auditors at hand; every night, for the *Zip* company, was election night, with John as the returning officer.

Then there was that other solid stand-by of the hard-working entertainer: pantomime. A decent summer show and a reasonable panto run more or less catered for one's bread and butter – if people just went twice a year to the theatre it was usually on seaside holiday and at Christmas. On Boxing Day 1957 John Wade made his pantomime debut at the Royalty Theatre, Chester. Given our interest in showbiz technology, it is worth a mention that the

Oh, no he didn't . . . John Wade as Simple Simon in his not so happy panto debut at Chester

Royalty was the first in the United Kingdom to have installed fluorescent stage lighting, which had the immense advantage of providing, at the touch of a switch, abrupt and immediate black-out. The best-laid electrical schemes being what they are, there was also the immense disadvantage of, when switching them on again, a disturbing phase of tremendous winking and flickering, familiar to all with such lights in kitchen or garage.

That stuttering illumination might have been an evil portent. John Wade did not enjoy his first panto, although he would later adjust to and appreciate the *genre*. This had nothing to do with his performance as the lead light comedian, Simple Simon in *Little Bo Peep*. That side of it was fine. The company rehearsed for a frantic week in London before the six-week Chester schedule, although with a script which included plentiful references to the performers' own material – John did his magic spot near the end of the show, inviting children up on stage as helpers in lieu of the conventional songsheet – possibly a week was not too desperate a period of preparation and the show went off without a hitch. Still, John Wade was a tad unhappy.

In the first place, he was not so well and, curse of the performer in winter, he could not jettison a dribbling cold and a hoarse cough, despite copious draughts of a patent remedy, Pulmo Bailey, well-known to 'pro's' as a creosote-tasting counter to ills, but probably long since banned by international scientific agreement because of its lethal ingredients. In the second place, he was a neophyte among a long-ordained priesthood. Even as a young contender among the summer show fraternity, he had felt he was allowed to toss in his four-penn'orth of suggestion, but panto was different. It was a carefully preserved and fondly hallowed set of rites and traditions. The temperamentally free-wheeling John Wade found it difficult to adjust to this elaborate and strict ritual. What may surprise the lay reader is that, finale garb apart, the principal artists had to provide their own costumes and some of the props, materials they had sacredly gathered and treasured as if churchly regalia. It was a trifle overpowering.

In the third place, there is anecdotal evidence over decades, if not centuries, to the shelter found in the theatre by social nonconformists, among them the lavishly effeminate, some of transsexual or homosexual leaning. Buffeted by the dismal moral and uptight legal disapproval of their host society, they had sometimes fled to the make-belief of on-stage and the solace of another reality backstage. Given its garish costuming and decor and its outrageous and cross-gender characterisation, the pantomime tradition possibly offered a particularly attractive locus for this mini-culture. John was not, even by the less tolerant standards of the 1950s, homophobic, but he did feel like an outcast on his own island. Many of the cast were drawn together in a clique which, after the fashion of oppressed minorities, communicated in its own *patois,* the 'Paloney' lingo made notorious, if – thankfully, from a Reithian viewpoint – untranslatable, by Kenneth Williams and Hugh Paddick as Julian and Sandy in the BBC radio programme, *Round the Horne.* There was no unkindness. There was no antagonism. There was, on John Wade's part, sheer unease. He felt like the oppressed minority.

He was only too pleased to return to the broader vistas of the London he loved in the late winter of 1958 and resume his nightly tryst with the freemasons and others foregathered in convivial functions, relieved to find himself again doing a proper job. By now John's father and mother were more reconciled to their only child's errant choice of career. It became their happy yearly practice to visit their son in his coastal habitat, usually managing to lodge with him, and to attend, with evident pride, the relevant summer show. The purchase of his first car in the late 1950s was a breakthrough. When he obtained this post-war symbol of steady and respectable social status, mother and father were appreciably more contented with John's progress. This happy conversion underlined the point that Amy and George Wade had been as bothered about the possibility of their son and heir's failure in an admittedly fragile profession as flustered by his outlandish choice of career.

There still hung over the relationship one unexplained secret. Right at the beginning of his career, as the retentive student of these pages will recall, John appeared in the *Rush-hour Revue* at London's Irving Theatre. One night, whilst on stage, he noted in the half-light of the auditorium, the familiar figure of his father perched on the end of the fifth row. At that point, with his parents opposed to his working on the stage, it was a vision he remarked with some astonishment. George Wade came and went, like the thief in the night, without a word before or since. Perhaps he had not told Amy Wade of his irresistible urge to take this esoteric peek at his local boy making good. Perhaps he did not quite understand what prompted him so to do. He never mentioned it to John and John never mentioned it to him. Funny things, parents.

Meanwhile, the conjuror's tale continued, with, around the corner, tumultuous events in both the personal and professional spheres. The Quixotic John Wade would soon be tilting at the Windmill in earnest.

Chapter Three
THE 1960s
FROM TIVOLI TO TELLY

That odd little *vignette,* with Wade *père,* playing the lead in 'the Silent Witness', reminds that, behind the tinselly pleasures of the proscenium arch, lurked personal and family affairs. Although this study is consciously about professional concerns, in chief, the spirited adaptability of our Just William anti-hero to the changing *milieux* of his trade, such everyday matters, of necessity, obtrude. Given that interaction of the public and private sectors of life, the most useful resolution is possibly to interpose a summary outline of John Wade's entire off-stage existence, before resuming the show-business analysis.

In 1955, at Torquay, a young, attractive soprano, Elizabeth Gordon, was on the bill. The only child of a well-established and well-to-do Salisbury family, she had studied singing and organ-playing at classical level, but, the calls for oratorio soloists being as rare as the mating cry of the Chinese panda, she turned to the popular stage. This was her first main booking and John's second summer show, and the two young performers became friendly; in fact, after something of a whirlwind romance, they married in October of that same year, honeymooning at a hotel at Babbacombe where they had, in the previous summer, spent precious free time wining and dining.

Tying the knot . . . the wedding of John Wade and Elizabeth Gordon. George Wade is on the extreme right and Amy Wade is second from the left

The newlyweds nested in a cosy flat behind Olympia in London, with Elizabeth proving a most efficient homemaker. The flat, incidentally, was the background for a sublime lesson in ragged-trousered philanthropy. The Wades were friendly with the double act, Chester Harriott and Vic Evans, two West Indian/Afro-American singers in the style of Layton and Johnstone. The economics of the entertainment industry are ever subject to sloughs in revenue flow and John Wade was forced to borrow a fiver off

Vic Evans to meet the rental on the flat. A month later, a little ashamed, he was still unable to repay the loan. Vic Evans was as philosophical as he was generous. 'Pass it on', he said. He explained that the honky-tonk pianist, Winifred Atwell, had loaned him a similar sum years before on the same condition, that he would, when better-heeled, assist the next generation of stragglers. 'Pass it on' is a sociable creed of very wholesome instincts, and one, by the by, to which John Wade has remained a strong adherent.

The stresses on show-business marriages are notoriously taut. Old Mother Riley and her daughter Kitty, at another stratum of reality the married couple, Arthur Lucan and Kitty McShane, led an uproarious life off-stage that all too precisely reflected their on-stage classic cameo. Entitled 'Bridget's Night Out', mother argued noisily with daughter, returning home late, with crockery smashed for good measure. It is a moot point as to whether nature was imitating art or the reverse, but theatre managements took a dim view of a turn that caused as much tumult back-stage as front-stage. The tale is told of that sophisticated act, the Western Brothers, in actuality, the cousins, Kenneth and George, being involved in a road accident and waking up in adjoining hospital beds, bandaged and splinted. 'At least, it's better', drawled George to Kenneth, 'than going on after Lucan and McShane.'

Of course, one could cite pairings of married artists who worked and lived together for years, like Robb Wilton and his wife and stage partner, Florence Palmer, or Anne Ziegler and Webster Booth. Nonetheless, there are peculiar stresses. Elizabeth's parents were, if only mildly, as perturbed by their daughter marrying a magician as John's parents had been at his becoming one, while Elizabeth herself was, naturally enough, uncertain about her own musical ambitions and whether Broadstairs was the right step towards the Royal Albert Hall. The newly-married Wades fell between two stools. While it was still, in the 1950s, the social fashion for married couples to be composed of a breadwinner and a *Hausfrau*, they were both careerists in their own right. On the other hand, they were not, *à la* Anne Ziegler and Webster Booth, a double act as such. They were, naturally, keen to work together and so they did. They 'Zipped' together at Broadstairs; indulged in 'Gaiety' at Minehead and 'Dazzled' in alliance at Cromer, while Elizabeth played Bo Peep, live sheep and all, to John's Simple Simon in Chester.

But this made them vulnerable to employers, ever keen to save a shilling or two, who booked them on dual contracts and lowered the joint offer, vowing that two may live as cheaply as one, in the knowledge that the twosome would probably take a flatlet for the season and self-cater. To some degree, it was the worst of both worlds. The nature of show-business can be very like the child's board game of Snakes and Ladders. Two discrete performers would be climbing up the ladders or tumbling down the snakes at differing times and points. Elizabeth, for instance, had lucrative television commercial engagements for a time, whereas, at other junctures, it would be John who spiralled upwards. Whatever the tug of living and working together, career paths beckoned differently.

The question of a family had, with both partners working, temporarily been shelved, not without some alarm in the bosoms of Elizabeth Gordon's parents, who, naturally enough, hoped for grandchildren. Bowing a little to such social pressures, along came David in 1962 and Lucy in 1964, to great joy and added complications. Several stage-door keepers, for instance, were tipped to keep an eye on a cradled David during his parents' theatrical appearances. In 1959 the couple had taken a deep breath and a largish mortgage, investing in a Chiswick house at a princely cost of £2800. It remains John Wade's base, although its value now is nearer £500,000. John's now ageing parents were settled in a flat at the top of the house, and, with work to be done and young children cared for, *aux pairs* were introduced into a crowded household. Strange how the 'servant' syndrome had missed a generation, a reflection, in particular, of the changing role of middle class women, from housekeeper to housewife to worker. In the event, George Wade died in 1962 and Amy Wade in 1965, happy in the knowledge that magicianship had not been the disaster they feared, but, to John's everlasting regret, not surviving long enough to enjoy him quite hit the high spots.

Eventually, Elizabeth would turn away from the entertainment business and become a successful music teacher in an exclusive Surrey girls' school, but, although the home was comfortable and the children well-cared for, there was, unavoidably, a drifting apart. It was scarcely helped by the fact that Elizabeth worked by day and John by night, a convoluted, unfunny Box and Cox misalliance. Elizabeth and John led increasingly separate existences. Eventually, years afterwards, Elizabeth moved to a family property in a lovely part of Cornwall, while David and Lucy, as far as this text is concerned, also moved on, for the unfolding of the ups and, unavoidably, downs of their own biographies. Maybe the Torquay holiday romance was not as deep-rooted as some relationships more fortunately are. Maybe the challenge of John's 'Excelsior' style ambition to climb ever upward caused some friction. Maybe, in the end, as in so many marriages, the Marxist Theory of Economic Determinism prevailed and there were arguments about money. Maybe, then, the differences could be summed up in three letters – £sd.

1968 was a critical year for John Wade in this bittersweet saga. He was offered a South African contract to front a touring company, including Senor Wences, the Spanish ventriloquist, who famously created a dummy from his hand, and with the Günther Kallman Choir topping the bill. Although it meant both professional and personal separation, John did not hesitate for a moment and off he went. It was hugely successful, playing for weeks in cities like Capetown and Pretoria, often with return dates, and inclusive of allied radio and other work. It was exciting and profitable, the first portent for John Wade of the extending boundaries of show-business overseas. And there was to be one of those coincidences that change destinies.

The lead singer in the famous German choir was a fetching redhead, Blanche Birdsong, her rare and pleasing surname celebrated in a street-name in downtown Longview, Texas, where her father, a sturdy builder, had been mayor. She followed in her mother's footsteps as a musician, training as a harpist at the Julliard School of Music in New York and then spending eight years with the City Centre Orchestra in that city. The leader of the Sauter Finnegan dance orchestra, Eddi Sauter, bethought himself to have a harpist in the ensemble, and recruited Blanche as the only woman in his band. Independent and liberal of mind, she had reacted against the redneck narrowness and McCarthyite intolerance of mid-century USA, and, touring with the dance band in Europe, she found the old world more to her liking. From 1957 the Sauter Finnegan 'big band' had a regular broadcasting engagement with the Sudwest Funk station in Baden Baden and Blanche settled in Germany. She married a German, a government public relations officer, and had a daughter, only to find her marriage, too, marooned on chilly rocks. Blanche became the lead singer of the Günther Kallman Choir and accompanied the choral group on its South African trip. John and Blanche met, the only two in the cast with English as their first language, and speedily fell in love. The civil servant's son from Eastcote, London and the bricklayer's daughter from Longview, Texas, were thrown together in South Africa. It is not overly syrupy to suggest they have been soul-mates these last 30-odd years.

Blanche Birdsong lived and lives in Koblenz. John Wade lived and lives in Chiswick. In cynically pragmatic terms, it may be easier, whatever the anguish of separations, to be soul-mates at a distance. Such a couple are able, when they meet, to concentrate on the grand spiritual and intellectual essentials, encouraging and counselling and comforting one another. Sometimes this seems less possible in the harder tack of household domesticity, with mortgage repayments, children's illnesses, worries over choice of schools, the spouting gutter, the unmown lawn and the unpainted spare room providing the day-by-day elements of dulling confrontation. One thinks, ineluctably, of St Luke, with Martha 'cumbered about much serving', while 'my sister hath left me to serve alone.' Although Mary, according to holy writ, 'hath chosen the good parts', there have been many devout Christians, faced with a sink full of greasy pots and pans, who have secretly sympathised with the application of Martha, even while admiring the virtue of Mary.

So much for amateur, if, one trusts, even-handed psychology. Whatever the case, John Wade is certain that it is about this time, and under Blanche's benign influence, that he felt liberated. Coupled with a startling leap in his professional credentials, he felt an immense sense of emancipation. The tussle, beginning with the negative family and school responses of his childhood and adolescence, had, to some extent, continued in his adult life. Now, for the first time, he was his own man, in that people – in particular, Blanche Birdsong – were telling him what he could do, what he was capable of, rather than what he could not and must not do.

Some educationists have argued that teachers tend to veer towards one or other end of a gamut of 'extenders' and 'distenders', the ones who lift or dampen confidence, the boosters and the crushers. You may feel, from a recollection of chapter one, that John Wade was peculiarly in need of an 'extender', such was his acute sensitivity to the unkind word and the wet blanket. You may be right. Nevertheless, it was a wondrous thing for him suddenly to sense that he was his own unique personality, one recognised and admired by others.

The 1960s had already delivered him a positive message along the same lines. He became a member of the London Savage Club in 1962. The Savage Club was established in 1857, after a convivial gathering at the Crown Tavern, Drury Lane, organised by the journalist, George Augustus Sala. It was formed as a Bohemian resort for impoverished penny-a-liners in the writing trade and those similarly struggling to make a crust in the artistic world. Some commentators have claimed that the Beargarden Club in Anthony Trollope's 1875 classical novel, *The Way we Live now,* is modelled thereon. The Savage Club preserves in large measure its reputation for welcoming such characters through its hospitable portals, just as, in perpetuity, it sustains its *danse macabre* between the red and black pigmentation of its accounts.

Some years ago the *Guardian* newspaper, in a feature on London clubs, bundled them into two groups, the 'silent' and the 'chatterbox'. John Wade's presence alone would ensure the Savage Club's placement in the latter category, but it has, in general, an enviable distinction for talkativeness. It is not a suitable locale for those of a taciturn disposition. As modern membership is steered by reference to six disciplines, art, music, law, science, theatre and literature, the resultant mix is a potent one. This is, in part, because specialists have other arrows in their quiver, so that the singing judge, as if auditioning for the Gilbert and Sullivan one-act comic opera, *Trial by Jury,* or the ophthalmologist-cum-clarinettist find there a perfect haven.

John Wade took to it like a duck to the water Savages occasionally add in minute quantities to their whiskies. He became and remained an ardent Honorary Life Member of The Magic Circle. Indeed, his magical qualifications — Gold Star Member of the Inner Circle of The Magic Circle, London and Honorary Member of the Academy of Magic Arts and Sciences, Hollywood, to mention but two — would choke with jealousy the average toiling academic, with his brace of moderate degrees and his clutch of arcane papers. Moreover, having no acquaintances from his younger days, he has formed firm friendships with other magicians, Alan Shaxon and Terry Seabrooke, to mention but two of many from among his magical peers. However, he turned more to The Magic Circle for professional reference, whereas the Savage Club became his central social focus.

It was something to do with widening his horizons and the necessity to seek non-magical, indeed, non-theatrical company. But perhaps the chief dimension of satisfaction was the feeling, in this interdisciplinary arena, that one was accepted at current face-values, as one's own person. The eminent surgeon, who thought nothing of his daily dalliance with life and death at the operating table, was lost in admiration at the skill of the brilliant fellow-member cartoonist. The violist, who took for granted his nightly parade of musical virtuosity on the concert platform, was baffled by and delighted at the ingenuity of the talented magician.

With the Savage Club, John Wade discovered, in a more congregational setting, what he would discover, more personally, more intimately, later in the same decade, with Blanche Birdsong; namely, what he might have defined, had he been so coolly analytical about it, as the inner core of his personality. He had, in Harold Laski's heartening phrase for the end-product of ethical socialism, 'realised his best self.' For 40 years the Savage Club has been for John Wade his watering-hole, his fount of what the Australians call 'mateness', and his outlet for a thousand examples of benevolent generosity, 'passing it on', as taught all those years before by Vic Evans.

Professionally, the 1960s were as big for John Wade as they were to be significant personally, although we must track back to 1959 for the salient incident. The televisual age was upon us. It was part of the 'miniaturisation' of society that witnessed a withdrawal of services into the home. For instance, the public wash-houses and commercial laundries were overwhelmed by the washing machine – two-thirds of households had one by the 1960s – whilst the central ice-stores, to the detriment, incidentally, of ice rinks, disappeared in the wake of the family fridge – barely 8% of families had one in the mid-1950s, but it leapt to 69% by the end of the

1960s. The television set was even more ubiquitous. The 5 million sets of the 1950s more than trebled by the end of the 1960s, by which time 90% of households had a telly. Moreover, they were well-used, with average weekly viewing pushing towards the twenty hours mark and with popular programmes harvesting audiences of as many as 20 millions. Theatre and cinema going, as estimated over visits in a preceding month, was down under 10%. The golden age of collective leisure was at an end.

Television was like an ancient deity that both destroys and renews, that both giveth and taketh away. As scores of theatres and cinemas, victims of the wrath of the Telly-god, echoed to the strident whine of the bingo caller, or were crushed before the thrust of the bulldozer, preparatory to a supermarket being erected on the site, other entertainment flourished at television's behest. In many ways it was ideal for acts like ventriloquists and conjurors, where an intense close-up focus heightened the pleasure and where the huge stage or radio (with, as we shall find, one very relevant exception) was not so fitting. It was rather like the different enjoyment of spectating live sport at a distance from the stands and watching it intently on the television from the armchair.

Furthermore, television was about the big battalions. When *King Lear* was first broadcast by the BBC on television, not many, by the exacting yardstick of the soap operas or major sports events, watched. Even so, at one fell swoop (to borrow from the bard's Scottish Play) they outnumbered all those who had ever watched a professional production of *King Lear* in Britain since it had been written almost 400 years previously. To take a modern example, the Football World Cup in 1998 was viewed by a quarter of the global population which, in turn, was 3% of all the human beings that have ever been born. Whatever else, television is important box office.

In December 1959 John Wade had had his moment. Actually, he had appeared on television as a schoolboy conjuror in a talent show called *New to You*, broadcast from Alexandra Palace, all orange face-pack and green lipstick and with the magic playing-cards curling visibly in the torrid heat of the concentrated lighting. He had also done his turn on *Miniature Music-hall*, a show broadcast about 5.30 pm, after the children's programmes and before their parents were ready to settle down for an evening's viewing. This was different. This was a week's magic show at the Scala Theatre, London, organised by The Magic Circle, and, something of a *coup* in itself, John Wade was cast in the role that became him aptly and one that he would regularly play; viz, the *compère* or MC. His insouciant style, unthreatening and friendly, with an easygoing touch of smiling humour, was tailor-made for the mastery of ceremonies. A quick, perplexing trick; a pithy one-liner or two, never hogging it, never overdoing it; a clean-cut introduction – and on with the show.

The BBC decided to televise it and, uncommonly for those days, they resolved to film and edit it, prior to later scheduling. Given John Wade's benign obsession with gadgetry, an appropriate trait in a magician, and given a general interest in the development of show-biz-technology, it is well worthy of mention that, during this shooting, John Wade became one of the first entertainers to utilise a precursor of the lapel microphone that hung round ones's neck on a string. The BBC had had to turn for this rare piece of filming over to its Outside Broadcasting Unit, and its commentators were, at that time, about the only ones using this pre-lapel mike with any seriousness.

Freed from being shackled to the standing microphone, and an arch-foe of the gob-sucking, hand-clutched contraption favoured by some comics and singers, John Wade was delighted. It suited his delivery admirably. At the same time, this smaller radio mike was at a primordial stage of its evolution. The microphone itself, strung around the throat, was the shape of an average cigarette lighter, while the transformer and the transmitter, each the size of an average cigarette packet, had to be secreted in pockets where normally billiard balls, thimbles and other magical impedimenta might be found. A ticklish aerial down the starboard trouser leg completed the circuit.

Once it was on, it stayed on, and, during the filming, John retired near the stage door to catch a breath of fresh air. A policeman entered the theatre, as policemen, keen to hobnob with the stars and have a quick smoke, were wont to do. This representative of the West End Division's finest was especially smitten by the lady magician, Rahnee Motie, a sorceress of tempting allure, who, awaiting her turn to perform, was standing within eyeshot. The police officer salaciously described to John, after the classic detection formula, his motive, method and wished-for opportunity, *apropos* the slaking of his animal desires. Then he spotted John Wade's mike and a countenance of puce became white. 'Is that on?' he gasped. 'Yes', answered John truthfully, and, turning to the sound recordist sitting with his assorted machinery nearby, asked 'did you get that?' He was monitoring all the input from several such mikes and his *bravura* thumbs-up dismayed the custodian of metropolitan justice. He imagined it was 'live' and that, even now, a shocked Commissioner, seeing the televised show in his New Scotland Yard office, was signing the errant officer's discharge papers.

A chastened bobby returned to tread his beat down a crowded Charlotte Street. For him it was back to normalcy. For John Wade it was lift-off. The edited highlights of the Scala entertainment, with John obviously much in evidence as the cheerful linkman, proved to be a major showcase for him. It abruptly tossed him on to a higher plateau of his profession. It was the considered opinion of many artists that a single premier (and, of course, successful) television appearance put a nought on one's fee . . . and so it proved. That factor of ten is quite a Weimar Republic inflation sort of increase, with, merely to emphasise the point, £10 for an evening's outing overnight worth £100. Sometimes only a *cliché* will suffice to tell the tale: so suddenly the telephone never stopped ringing.

On average John's weekly dates jumped from eight to 12, meaning that, some days, he was doing two or even three spots or gigs. Moreover, the bookings were better paid and John Wade could only rue the fact that his 1960 summer contract at Ilfracombe was, unfortunately, already signed and sealed. But next year beckoned. Company directors who had witnessed him on TV were contacting agents with instructions to book John for this or that business function. Again, where he had chiefly operated, the summer apart, in and around London, he now expanded to a national ambit.

An interesting aspect of this was invitations to entertain at political conferences and rallies, or maybe at select meals – for Harold Wilson, for instance, at a small dinner party at Llandudno in the party conference season. At an Edinburgh Labour rally John Wade did a warm-up piece prior to an address by Jim Callaghan, who began his speech, with a veracity devastating in a politician, 'I know you'd rather watch the conjuror.' Murmured acerbically-tongued Clive Jenkins, the mercurial white-collar union leader, to John, 'trust him not to mention your name.' It has to be said that John Wade was not imbued by these experiences with any fondness for politicians of whatever persuasion. He would echo the comment of David Broder, the American political critic, writing in the *Washington Post* in 1973, 'anybody that wants the presidency so much that he'll spend two years organising and campaigning for it, is not to be trusted with the office.'

For the next few years the work was non-stop and profitable, very much seven days a week, with a proliferation of Sunday concerts. The class of work, the venues, that is, and the quality of the co-stars, rose precipitately. With all due respect to the Marcia Owens and Jerry Jeromes, to the Cromers and Westgates, now we discover ourselves visiting Jersey at St Helier's largest theatre in company with Billy Cotton and his ebullient band-show, or off, in 1967, for a season in Blackpool, the peak summer ambition of every entertainer. The Blackpool summer took the form of an itinerant show with the singer, Denis Lotis, pursuing a set of busy nightly venues, but with all the brash flavour of that outgoing resort, rubbing shoulders with Cilla Black, Adam Faith and the other celebrities who were then the aristocrats of the capital of the show-business kingdom. Or we now join John for classy bookings along with the Latin American rhythms of Edmundo Ros, while there was also cabaret in urbane night clubs, with night spots like the Blue Angel providing a somewhat different setting for John than, say, a Masonic Ladies' Evening in Fulham.

Let us look more closely at some of these excitements. The summer of 1965 found John Wade enjoying a long season working for Sandy Powell in Eastbourne, where that favourite child of Rotherham had, through his continuum of annual appearances, earned the nickname of 'Mr Eastbourne.' Old hands will recall that he offered two fabled skits, the 'cod' ventriloquist, in which he tried to persuade his dummy to hail from Leeds rather than the unpronounceable Wolverhampton, and the 'cod' conjuror. He delighted in tendering the latter contribution soon after John had done his turn, the burlesque following the genuine article, just as the 'cod' monologist, Billy 'Almost a Gentleman' Bennett, in former days, would succeed the straight actor, perhaps trumping his *The Green Eye of the Little Yellow God* with the ace of his own parody, *The Green Tie on the Little Yellow Dog*. Sandy Powell was one of the first to coin a radio catch-phrase, 'Can you hear me, mother?', allegedly what he spontaneously said when asked for voice-level on his first visit to Broadcasting House. Years later he pursued his 'vent' act into his eighties, frequently playing in, for instance, clubs where some of the clientele were either too youthful, intoxicated or unintelligent to recognise a lampoon when gifted one. His response to drunken hecklers was Delphic. In reply to the accusation, 'I can see your lips move', he remarked darkly, 'Aye, but only when the dummy's speaking.'

John Wade often worked with Sandy Powell. Once, prior to a Sunday concert at Bexhill, they were having a meal together on the promenade. 'I was in this very cafe three Sundays ago', began Sandy Powell, in his gravely tones. 'It was exactly the same; egg, beans and chips, and the deck chairs blowing down the prom, when this couple walked in and the man spotted me and thought he recognised me.' Sandy Powell then reconstructed the antics of this amnesiac fan as he struggled to recall his hero's name, rather like Tony Hancock in his famous army reunion sketch. There was the finger jabbing in desperation and the hand clutching frustratedly at the forehead, along with urgently whispered 'no, don't tell me's', as the name slid towards the tip of the tongue, only to slide away again. Eventually the triumphant dawn of identification dawned across his face. 'I've got you,' he yelled, 'you've said it a thousand times and you'll be saying it up there again tonight . . . 'the day war broke out . . .'. The information had obviously eluded him that Robb Wilton no longer haunted the Dog and Pullet, having sadly died in 1957. No more would he pause in horror at the memory of his wife, Rita, suggesting that he would 'have to get work': seconds would elapse before he would lugubriously reflect, 'ee, she's a cruel tongue, that woman.'

A Channel Island summer with Billy Cotton was another grand and remunerative experience. John Wade did his act in the first half, together with the Television Toppers and Mrs Mills, who had transformed pub piano playing into a minor science. John acted as *compère* and thus it was his nightly task to introduce Billy Cotton's show band which occupied the whole of the second half. 'Ladies and gentlemen', he would cry, 'welcome Billy Cotton' – and up from the band-leader would go the *reveille*-style call, redolent of barrack-room and holiday camp, 'Wakey Wakey!', the signal for a tumultuous onslaught on *Somebody Stole My Girl,* the musical accompaniment for many years to the Sunday roast beef and Yorkshire pud of a generation.

Although Billy Cotton was noted as a generous employer in a field where some of his fellow-conductors were a trifle on the miserly side, he also had a quick temper and anecdote told of one errant musician unceremoniously sent crashing, Mack Sennett-like, through a drum-kit in consequence of this heatedness. It came to John's aid during this season. The show lacked a comedian and the management, anxious about the low decibel count of laughter in the first half, began to press John Wade unfairly under this heading. This proved too much for Billy Cotton, who put an end to such a whispering campaign with withering contempt, loudly scornful of a management which was too mean to book a comic. That was the gist of his argument. Its lurid supporting embroidery may not prudently be detailed in a work that may fall into the hands of children or those of a nervous disposition.

This was at a time when Billy Cotton was recovering from a severe stroke and was supposed to be avoiding upset. 'He's supposed to keep quiet', murmured his awestruck singer, Kathie Kay, during this particular tirade. It was her job to drive the recuperative Billy Cotton, something which, as a one-time motor cycle and racing car driver, he hated. One day, John Wade, with Mrs Mills his passenger, passed the band-leader and his melodious *chauffeuse*, at quite a steady lick on the narrow winding lanes of St Helier between hotel and theatre. At curtain call that night, John heard the whispered query in his ear, 'how long did that ride take you today, son?'. Rather taken aback by both the poser and the setting, John answered, 'oh, about fifteen minutes.' Later that evening Kathie Kay anxiously asked John, 'what have you said to him? He's like a bear with a sore head.' Come the following evening's performance and, once again, John found himself next to Billy Cotton at the final curtain, with *I've got a Lovely Bunch of Coconuts* at full blast. Billy Cotton always carried his famed bass drum. As John Wade smiled and bowed, he felt himself goosed by the conductor's drumstick and heard the muttered comment from the purportedly banned driver, 'twelve minutes, son, twelve minutes.'

It even fell to John Wade to conduct one of Britain's most popular bands ever. Billy Cotton was filming throughout the season for his TV series and one episode involved an exploding piano. The explosives were foolishly overestimated and Alan Breeze, Billy Cotton's versatile vocalist, ended up with a back out of which John Wade had to pick pianoforte shrapnel, whilst Billy Cotton himself was temporarily deafened. That night he placed John Wade on the front row of the stalls to follow the tempo of the band with a discreetly moving finger, so that Billy Cotton, on stage, had a digital prompt to ensure that his conducting was synchronised with the music.

These were heady days, fondly recalled by John Wade. He was in variety in bracing Skegness, for instance, with George Martin, 'the Casual Comedian', noted for his relaxed manner and his topical gags, a man who later, by coincidence, was to be involved with the David Nixon magic TV programmes, as well as helping to make Basil Brush a household name. The Tanner Sisters were also on the bill, while, down the promenade, Peter Sellers topped another bill, assisted by Michael Bentine and the Malcolm Mitchell Trio. It was realised that all these artists were ex-RAF and the resultant *camaraderie* led to reciprocal practical jokes, which, at one performance, John Wade, when he advanced from backstage at the finale of his act to float a shining sphere spectacularly, found his ankles held through the rear curtains by Peter Sellers, who had smuggled himself into the theatre. Both sets of players descended on a bemused RAF camp nearby, with a total complement of only 30 personnel, in order to provide a late evening's entertainment that rocked on until the wee hours – and which John Wade, typically, the compere for this *ad libretto* extravaganza, describes as just about the most riotously funny night he has ever known.

The ramifications were ever-extending, as if that Scala TV appearance had been the pebble tossed into the pond, with the consequent endless ripples. There was radio, a medium in which John Wade, the gab-gifted John Wade, proved to be extraordinarily adept, just as Peter Brough, with Archie Andrews, demonstrated, in the BBC long-running series, *Educating Archie,* that ventriloquism might conquer the air waves. John's fast-talking descriptions of tricks, including the time when he sawed in half the popular disc jockey, Pete Murray, began in 1968 and, in 1969, John had a weekly radio slot for a 13-week series – and he is still invited to do occasional work of this kind.

The radio interest arose through an invitation from the BBC producer, Richard Willcox, to talk on *Late Night Extra* about the vicissitudes of going to work when most sane people were going to bed. John Wade asked if he could do a trick as well to enliven the proceedings and, although slightly bemused by the alien concept, Richard Willcox agreed. This proved very popular. Operationally, it worked most effectively when there was a helpmate in the studio who was self-evidently not a stooge, a fellow guest, such as a bishop or judge, being ideal, while another gimmick was to phone someone at home and use him or her as assistant. Next John began to choose his own guests, well-known entertainers like Jimmy Edwards, Ruby Murray or Dickie Henderson.

On one occasion John Wade left a banana under a pint glass in the studio and set forth in a radio car to the headquarters of The Magic Circle, with Val Doonican as his guest accomplice. The singer was invited to peel a banana and, equipped with a knife, asked to cut it into sections. He sliced it into three pieces. The presenter back in the studio was then commanded to remove the banana from its transparent confines and to peel it. It fell into three sections. The announcer was completely flabbergasted and inadvertently gasped, 'well, if anyone can tell me how John Wade did that . . .' Thousands responded to the challenge, as if Billy Cotton had roused them with his clarion appeal of 'Wakey Wakey!'. The BBC switchboard was jammed and, the following week, the producer, uncertain whether to laugh or cry, took John silently into his office and opened a cupboard packed with various items of fruit, each of them at some phase of decomposition, as well as neatly divided into a varying number of sections.

John Wade caused one other blockage of the corporation's long-suffering telephones. This was as a result of one of his several appearances on Pete Murray's morning programme, *Open House.* It was one of those infuriatingly numerate tricks, with an Einsteinian formula, along the lines of think of a number, double it, multiply by five, take away the number you first thought of and the end-product is your age and your shoe size. The BBC was besieged for copies of the routine, so much so that a printed leaflet had to be made available to the public. And each radio spot was, of course, a further advertisement for the affable magic-man.

A further example was BBC's *Roundabout*, on which John Wade joined the lanky, amiable John Dunn for a regular twice weekly two minute slot in the late 1960s. As well as having a magical flavour, these spots reflected John's extensive travels, including broadcasting from a nuclear submarine at Gibralter, from the footplate of *The Flying Scotsman* on a special trip to York, from East Berlin through Checkpoint Charlie and from the first hovercraft plying between Southsea and the Isle of Wight.

There was television. In 1968 John Wade appeared in the show in which, if only partially, more people were to see him than in any other, and in their veritable millions. He was to be viewed in *The Avengers,* with Patrick MacNee starring as the polished John Steed, alongside Tara King, played by Linda Thorsen, who had replaced Diana Rigg as his sophisticated sidekick, Emma Peel. It was a cult show, which somehow brokered mayhem and violence against a sheen of *politesse.* The producer, Brian Tesler, asked John Wade to give a stylish background to the credits. Practically everyone who watched *the Avengers* recollects the title credits, with their peacock-feathered array of rapidly changing displays of playing cards. The avenging couple were epitomised in the credits by a masculine bowler hat, with a feminine string of pearls lying nonchalantly across it. At the last the cards are squirted, evenly and flowingly, into the bowler hat. The hands and the cards belonged to John Wade, his trademark trickery captured for many repeats and for all time. John managed the cascade into the hat at the first attempt and modestly refused the opportunity of a second take.

As in the case of the televised King Lear, more people saw John Wade's fingers at their adept work then ever saw Houdini live. *The Avengers* has been screened in 89 countries. It makes for a curious example of anonymous identity, for, in an odd kind of way, it formed the apex of John Wade's career. The eyes of millions who could not tell you his name gleam with remembrance when those credits are described. One immediate benefit was that it created other opportunities for John on television when conjuring was in demand. For example, he was requested to perform the three-card trick on four or five occasions, either whole, as the actor, or in part, that is, just the hands. Next time you watch a repeated episode of *The Saint, Doctor in the House* or *Minder*, there is a chance you may see John Wade gulling mock victims with his confidence trickery.

In *The Saint* he found himself for real in the Portobello Road early in the morning. There he was in a doorway, with suitcase and small plank, simple accoutrements that could rapidly be dissembled should the law intervene. The cockney character actor, Alfie Bass, was the 'shill', the plant who, by winning, encourages the mugs to risk their hard-earned. He was very taken by the number of locals who were crowding around with the paid extras, suggesting to John that they might 'make their lunch money' if John, in the most realistic sense, played his cards right. They went for a take, with Ian

Ogilvy, as Simon Templar, on hand to join the scene. John, wearing a microphone inside his sweater, began his Del-boy spiel. There were three lots of police in the vicinity: the regular beat constables; a traffic unit hired by the TV company to keep the roadways clear; and the costumed actors, conspicuous by the length of their hair. It was all too much for one of the bystanders. John was suddenly conscious of a man behind him at his shoulder, hissing into the mike. 'Piss off, the Bill's here', then vanishing with an alacrity most magicians might envy. What with the policeman at the Scala Theatre and now this denizen of Portabello Road, John was contriving to record for posterity all sides of the juridical system. However, he surely had a right to be proud of the authenticity of his performance.

There was the Windmill. The Windmill, opened with its *tableaux* of still nakedness in 1932 by Vivian Van Damm, had something of a war-time *ambience,* with stationary nudes defiant in the face of the Luftwaffe, and then with its small stage offering a vital fanlight, scarcely a window, of opportunity for demobbed would-be comedians. The likes of Tony Hancock, Tommy Cooper, Harry Secombe, Bruce Forsyth, Peter Sellers, Alfred Marks, Harry Worth, Michael Bentine . . . *et al* all queued up at 'the Comic's Dunkirk'. They learned their trade the hard way, fighting to attract the attention of a mute assembly of rain-coated males, anxious for the return of immovable nudity, and it comes as no surprise to learn that it was at the Windmill where Jimmy Edwards honed his raucous catch-phrase, 'Wake up at the back there.' However, the show persisted into the 1960s, and John Wade was booked for his first season there in 1963 and thereafter did several short seasons. It was a tough assignment, involving five or six performances a day.

In 1964, the Windmill, forfeiting its intransigent boast, closed. John Wade, who had been booked by the Bernard Delfont Office, was selected to be the very last act on the very last show ever at the Windmill, a daunting occasion, given that the audience was a hand-picked *ensemble* of former Windmill *habitués,* many of them by now established stars. The theatre was packed and so were the streets around, with television units mingling with the crowds and with John and the other performers feeling rather hemmed in by the gathering. John hired a little telly, just half a crown (12.5p) for the week, hung it up in the dressing room and watched all the activity inside and outside the theatre. His act went well and, as the final fan-dancer provocatively adjusted the ultimate fan, the stars assembled on stage and the champagne corks popped. After 'The Man who Shot Liberty Vallance' and 'The Man they couldn't Hang', John Wade was able to add to his billing, had he so wished, 'The Man who Closed the Windmill.'

Throughout the late 1950s and into the bustling 1960s John Wade had still not been represented by a single agent, but had remained on the books of several. He had been contacted for variety bookings by the Joe Collins agency, a sound, medium-sized outfit with a Soho office. It was on his visits thither that John would occasionally meet one of Joe's daughters, Joan. Joan Collins, in John's estimation a very smart lady indeed, was already shining brightly as a star in the firmament, where she was certainly clever enough to avoid the rapid extinction visited on many in the show-business galaxy. It is another yardstick of John Wade's ascent that he shared an agent and, on occasion the tiny rickety lift to his Soho eyrie, with Joan Collins and Petula Clark.

'As known . . .'; that was the telling phrase in Joe Collins' contracts or anybody else's. The contract would state the date, place, timing and salary, but all 'as known'. It was a significant proviso. It obliged the artist to trot out what conventionally was his material, the content, be it songs, dialogue or tricks, by which he was generally known. It protected against two dangers. On the one hand, it prevented a performer from abruptly introducing unproven or alien matter, with, for example, John Wade suddenly doing a dog act. On the other hand, it ensured that performers would offer the public that which was familiarly expected of them. It guaranteed, in illustration, against Donald Peers, perhaps tiring of his babbling brook, allowing it to dry up, the shady nook abandoned, and the audience devastated. Donald Peers' brook was not unlike Tennyson's poetic brook: 'for men may come and men may go, but I go on for ever.'

There was nightlife. During the 1960s the nightclubs were numerous and well-populated, with gambling very much a part of the swinging metropolis. There was an emphasis on exotic femininity; indeed, one reason why the Windmill lost impact was that the Lord Chamberlain's rule remained sacrosanct and thus the nudes remained stationary in the theatres, whereas the private clubs, with, ostensibly, entry allowed only to members, enjoyed some laxity in this respect, that is, the nudes were, so to say, upwardly mobile. Nonetheless, there remained a clientele that also enjoyed what were called 'talking acts', among which John Wade was pleasingly numbered. Midnight and afterwards would find him chatting, thimbling and mirroring in such resplendent locations as the Edmundo Ros Club, Regent Street; the Embassy, Bond Street; the Churchill Club, Mayfair or the Blue Angel, Berkeley Square, with David Frost fronting the show and with co-stars like the velvet-toned Hutch or, with topical verses at the piano, Paddy Roberts.

Eventually it was to be a fading scene. The clubs sold out, many of them to Middle Eastern purchasers, and the accent became even more pronounced on the gambling and the sexuality. The freeing up of the licensing laws permitted the pubs to stay open longer and, in turn, this pushed back the time at which the night clubs became a popular option. The 'talking acts' went out of fashion. John Wade had a close-hand experience of this change. One club owner, thwarted by the wastefulness of premises scarcely utilised until after midnight, decided to open for business earlier with a cabaret and some music, and John was summoned to provide the entertainment. A three piece ensemble played peaceful airs and

John did his act to what, in the then graphic showbusiness epithet, was known as 'two poofs and a postman', its vividness some compensation, perhaps, for its wild political incorrectness. Then the owner and John settled down for a conversation over a bottle of Scotch, and the time, as it is wont to do, passed. The next time John peered out at the auditorium there were two dozen musicians raising orchestral Cain and two hundred punters dining, wining, betting and being propositioned. 'All they want', said the owner sadly, 'is a hostess and a plate of hash'. It was at this juncture that the provincial mind of John Wade's faithful recordist had to be disabused of the understanding that this was of a similar recipe to the thousand plates of hash he had consumed at Tuesday dinner-time throughout his northern childhood in the 1930s.

Nightlife made for some quaint engagements. There was the one at Bognor Regis, for example, where the wrestling promoters thought that acts between the bouts would be a fillip, and John Wade, for the only time in his career, ducked between the ropes of the ring and trod the sprung canvas. Then he was invited to do a week at the Jack of Clubs, situated below Jack Isow's restaurant in Soho's Brewer Street. Actually, it was a day less than a week. Ominously, the booked conjuror had been sacked precipitately after his first appearance on the Monday. The club tended to cater for a dubious fraternity, one that floated indeterminately on the surface not far above the underworld and John protested that this hard gambling clientele was unlikely to be much interested in his genteel charms. He was persuaded to try out the Tuesday and, as he was received with respectful attention, if not obeisant adulation, he returned for the rest of the week.

On the Thursday he arrived soon after midnight, parked his car by the doorway and skipped down the stairs. He was halted by Nosher Powell, no relation to Sandy. Nosher was a somewhile stuntman, bit-part actor in the roughshod henchman category and presently bouncer at the Jack of Clubs. He button-holed John with a sure literalness, grasping a chunk of his dinner jacket in his thick fist and drawing him closer for ease of communication. ''Ere, son', he began, 'you like to be a bit cheeky, don't you, chatting to the punters, and that.' John felt obliged to agree. 'Well, tonight – don't look, don't talk, go straight home'. John again felt no urge to demur, but Nosher was not yet satisfied that the message had been received and understood. He pulled John a little closer and, what with his own height and the advantage of the upper stair, Nosher towered a couple of feet above him: 'no, listen, son – don't look, don't talk, go straight home.'

John Wade entered the precincts of the club to discover a subdued atmosphere. The five piece band was playing without gusto, their heads never lifted from the music stands. The eight skimpily clad dancers ventured on stage; there was no reaction. They returned to the wings, their glassy eyes now matching their frozen smiles. An under-the-breath blasphemous imprecation was their only way of releasing the tension after what had been an arduous essay in the Terpsichorean art. On went John Wade, the new not looking, not talking John Wade. He became dimly aware that amid what the hymnist called the encircling gloom there were, as well as the usual scatter of small tables, two large tables, right and left of front centre, at which groups of large men were seated. They were talking quietly and drinking steadily, but then they began to remark the young conjuror. Suddenly one of the tables broke out in a collective guffaw at one of John's tricks. It was not the sort of laughter a performer wishes to hear. It was the sort of laughter which proclaimed that here was a bright young entertainer and we understand what he's about because we're smarter than the bunch at the other table. At the next sally, like a well-rehearsed claque, the other table bellowed even more loudly, exhibiting the strength of their accumulative IQ's. So the tourney of mirthless laughter continued, each table trying to outdo the other in its intellectual appreciation, and with the chilly waters of fear swishing metaphorically around the hapless magician's ankles. John Wade condensed his leisurely gavotte of 20 minutes into an eight minutes gallop; like the investigative journalists of the era, crime reporting for such organs as the *News of the World* or the *Sunday People,* he 'made an excuse and left'; rushed to the car and sped away home.

On the Friday evening Nosher Powell was waiting on the stairs for him. He grinned admiringly. 'You done well, son', he admitted. 'You didn't look; you didn't talk and you went straight home . . . there was a knifing 20 minutes after you left.' Apparently there had been a double booking of some consequence. The Kray gang, criminal lords of the East End, had been at one table and their arch-enemies, the Richardsons, the South London crime-kings, had been at the other. They stood in a felonious lineage that stretched back to medieval times, encompassing, for instance, Dick Turpin and 'the Essex Gang' in the 1730s and – another nefarious Montague/Capulet parallel – the Whites of Islington and the Billy Hill mob of Seven Dials in the 1940s. The atmosphere in the Jack of Clubs had not been unlike a scene from the spoof prohibition film, *Robin and the Seven Hoods,* made, coincidentally, in 1964, with Frank Sinatra and Peter 'Columbo' Falk as the rival gang bosses; similar, that is, until the real-life trouble began.

After the celebrated 1968 tour of South Africa, John Wade embarked on two consecutive prestigious tours. One was organised by the *Daily Mirror,* raising the newspaper's profile around the seaside resorts. A huge fit-up arena was transported from venue to venue, weeks about, and erected on the beach. John Wade hosted a game show for the holidaymakers, with lots of happy-go-lucky stunts, puzzles and prizes, chiefly cameras. *Mastermind* it wasn't: blowing up a balloon while eating a cream cracker was par for this particular obstacle course. It was a busy, successful and profitable summer. After the final show at Scarborough the student gang responsible for upping and downing the mobile rig were minded to erect it on the South Mimms roundabout by way of celebration.

The other tour was with the famous Fol-de-Rols concert party. It starred the comic, Jack Tripp, and the comedienne, Joan Mann, the wife of the show's organiser, Hugh Charles. Again it was a very successful set of outings. It was during this second tour that John appeared at the New Theatre, Cardiff, the week following the inauguration of Prince Charles as Prince of Wales at Caernarfon. He was, inevitably, the *compère*, making his entrance at the beginning of the show down a long Scarlett O'Hara staircase through an entire company of colleagues in powdered wigs and knee breeches. With Cardiff freshly bedecked in bilingual signs, John learned some Welsh phrases for friendly starters – only to discover half-way through his pigeon Welsh introduction that the auditorium was packed with 2000 American tourists, already struggling with the convoluted concepts of Fol-de-Rols in an 18th century drawing-room.

Summer tours; variety and cabaret; television; radio; nightclub: this was an extremely hectic time in John Wade's life. A typical day, or rather night, might have followed this frantic pattern. Nine o'clock: an after-dinner gig, perhaps for a Masonic evening, maybe at Simpsons' Restaurant on the Strand. Eleven o'clock: entertainment at what would now be called a corporate function, at, say, the Park Lane or Grosvenor Hotel. One o'clock: cabaret at a night club, such as the Blue Angel.

The money rolled in, not in the shovel-fulls that were being picked up by the major stars, those, usually now recording artists, with a stellar reputation, but rolling in very pleasantly. Each of the two once-off appearances each night might have brought in £10 each, while the nightclub was a guaranteed £50 a week. This was a seven days a week commitment, and the likelihood of those paired early bookings was strong. It meant something in the region of £200 a week, which, with lots of extras from daylight work, tours and the new-found opportunities of the media, grew once, at its very peak, to an annual income of approximately £12,000. Then came the

Sorcery and Senior Citizenry . . . John Wade entertains Swanley old age pensioners in 1967

unforgettable moment in the unlikely setting off a Wellingborough factory, appearing with Peter Goodwright and the Beverley Sisters at a large company event. It was John Wade's first £100 cheque for one appearance.

A more normal and ordinary financial year was that of 1964/65, meticulously recorded by John Wade in a simple exercise book, ready for his accountant to practise upon the figures his own peculiar sleight of hand. The annual total was £2265, although, John disarmingly confesses, a couple of cash-in-hands might have somehow remained unsung in these hand-written annals. That was a very steady income for a white-collar worker of the day, but the intriguing aspect is more the provenance of the income. It is the range and the gradual accumulation of varied items that is interesting. There is £30 a week for the Southsea season, but John was also booked through that summer to appear every Sunday at the Bognor Lido, at £7 a time. Other Sunday concerts drew in as much as £20 each, while television adverts brought approximately £100 to the Wade exchequer. Although never primarily a children's entertainer, John Wade joined Roy Castle in a series of ten trips to children's residential homes. This tour was organised by the Variety Club of Great Britain in the wake of the dreadful Thalidomide problem that left so many children disabled. It netted John a modest £6 for each such visit, while old age pensioner parties earned an even more humble two or four guineas, the survival of that once dignified coin itself a curio in the purportedly dynamic 1960s.

Some measure of John Wade's economy becomes clearer. It is the economy of a popular, well-respected, entirely reliable, middle-of-the-bill act, lending top-ranking support to, say, the Sandy Powell managed Eastbourne show at £45 a week, Billy Cotton's extravaganza at £35 a week, the Blue Angel nightclub at £35 a week, and the Windmill at £45 a week – with an extra fiver for the close-down week. It is basically the same act or set of glosses on the same act, but the fees earned differ considerably.

Let us try all that on for size, as previously, against the salaries of professionals of the same age, that is, in their mid to late 30s. During the 1960s the up and coming university lecturer or local government officer, half way up the promotional ladder, would have been content with a half of that. Readers will recollect that, the last time we attempted this confessedly rule-of-thumb comparison, John Wade was barely keeping up with the *bourgeois* pack, Now he was outstretching them, at least in the best years, by a substantial amount, but, needless to say, they would soldier on and ever upward, buoyed by the near certainties of the agreed salary scale and its cosy increments. For John Wade and his colleagues it was a question of coining it while one could, for, as *Gone with the Wind* reminds us, tomorrow is another day. Whether it was gathering rosebuds while ye may or making hay while the sun shone,

Commercial Breaks . . . John Wade prepares a TV advert for Magnet Ales

only the present had, economically speaking, any meaning. It was a mood which chimed in with the furious pace of the 1960s.

The benchmarks of the 1960s have only to be catalogued to remind one of the feverish and ephemeral mood of those times, those fast-moving years of transient and sometimes hollow happenings. They embraced the Lady Chatterley case in 1959; the 1963 Great Train Robbery; the Profumo Affair, featuring Stephen Ward and Christine Keeler, in the same year; the 1966 Moor Murders trial and the Kray Brothers, doubtless refreshed by their evening of prestidigitation at the Jack of Clubs, on trial in 1969. Crimes of violence had soared from under 6000 in 1955 to over 20,000 in 1968. More pertinently for our immediate concerns, theatre censorship was abolished in 1968. There were vivid slashes of cultural gesticulation, like the Premium Bonds, forerunner of the National Lottery; and the unshackling of gambling; Beatlemania; Flower-Power; and the Permissive Society, with the Pill, used by a fifth of married couples under 45 by the 1960s, its main catalyst.

Where the great reforms of preceding progressive administrations, in the 1870s, the 1900s and the 1940s, had tended to be collectivist, as in the fields of health, housing, education or welfare, the liberal legislation of this epoch was largely individualistic, ridding the nation of repressive laws on abortion, divorce and homosexuality and halting the ancient nastiness of capital punishment. Possibly the only lasting institutional feature of what is sometimes scathingly termed 'sixties socialism' is the Open University. Many of those emblems of the 1960s now appear a trifle woebegone. For example, the much-hyped satire of the 1960s was rather soft-centred and a television series like *That was the week that was* now looks more self-indulgent than, as it was perceived, shockingly extravagant.

From the entertainer's angle the good news was that full employment was maintained and income was high enough to warrant the title of the Affluent Society being bestowed on the nation. In the early 1950s, as John Wade was dipping his toe in the theatrical waters, the average adult weekly wage was just over £8; by the end of the 1960s, with John at the sovereign pinnacle of his career, it was touching £30. There was inflation, but there was a also a proportionate decrease in the cost of many items, and average weekly earnings rose sharply by as much as 134% between 1955 and 1969. Motor cars were one of the consumer products which, *pro rata,* were dropping in price. John Wade himself had, to his parents' contentment, as we have previously noted, joined the automotive throng, the car being absolutely essential for his rapid professional transit.

The 2.3 million vehicles of 1950 became, phenomenally, the 11.8 million vehicles of 1970. As John opened in his summer show at Cromer in 1959, the first stretch of the M1 was opened, whilst, during the 1960s, domestic air traffic doubled from 1000 million to 2000 million passenger kilometres. There was money to be spent and places to visit and methods of travelling to them. John bought a new car in Clacton. It had its then customary 250 miles service after two days and its 3000 miles service by the end of the week. He was averaging over 30,000 miles driving a year. It is an apposite moment to contemplate the loneliness of the long distance conjuror, or, to be more exact, the solitude of the solo performer. It is perhaps difficult for the majority of ordinary nine-to-fivers to appreciate the psychological tempo imposed by a working life that contrasted fifteen minutes of highly concentrated intensity in the public glare with hours of driving, often through deserted, darkened streets, with just oneself for company.

However, for bright, sharp-eyed entertainers, like John Wade, who kept physically mobile and socially flexible, there were rich pickings in these years. One way and another, then, the 1960s swung for John Wade. This was very much his decade, as he himself moved through his personal thirties. In professional entertainment, as in professional sport, the successful performer's career describes something of a parabola, moving upwards through the apprenticeship and the salad days, peaking over the upper arc of the curve and, inevitably, slowing a little and falling away in later years. For John the 1960s were definitely the golden years. There was, as shall be revealed, plenty of honey left in the pot in the 1970s, but, for sheer, enthralling engagement at the top of his profession, to say nothing of solid earning power, as Mary Hopkin's lyric of the era ran, 'those were the days, my friend.'

It is not remarkable that the decade in which John Wade found personal fulfilment and buoyant maturity was the one in which he found maximal professional satisfaction. The one hoisted the other in a rising spiral of achievement.

But, wait, there is often a hazard around the next corner.

THE COLOURFUL JOHN WADE

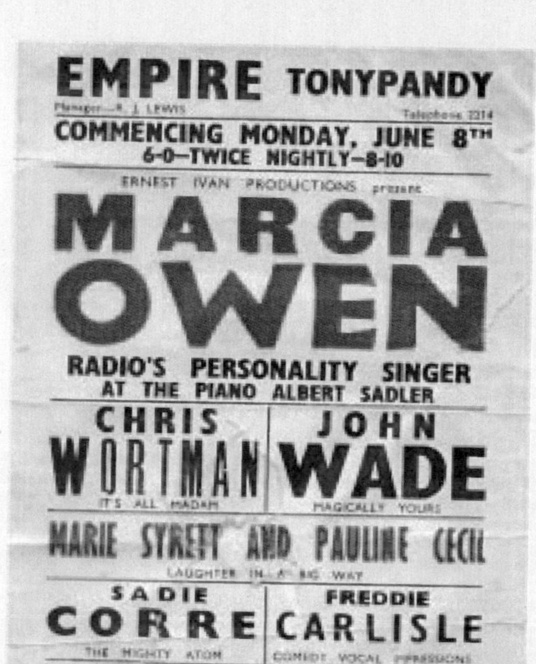

Breakthrough . . .
♦ John Wade's first variety billing and . . .

♦ his first major TV success from the Scala Theatre, London

Development . . .

♦ John Wade enjoys top billing with his conjuring peers and. . .

♦ stars in the musical extravaganza, *The Music Man*

Consolidation . . . John Wade in
♦ the BBC's long-running *The Good Old Days* from the Leeds City Varieties;

♦ as a gambler in a once-off episode of *The Late Late Show*, and . . .

♦ in his own one-man show in Hertfordshire

Culmination . . .
John Wade
♦ fund-raising for a cause he knows about only too well

Arthritis Care has some tricks up its sleeve . . .

We can offer people with arthritis and their families practical advice and information, support and friendship. We really understand.

IF YOU NEED US – JOIN US.
IF YOU CAN HELP US – VOLUNTEER.

♦ John Wade's proproom . . . the Wizard's Den, tidied up for the occasion

♦ at ease at Paul Daniel's house, relaxed in Houdini's favourite chair from the old Magicians' Club

Chapter Four
THE 1970s
CRUISES AND CRISES

'. . . As you glide effortlessly through the sun drenched sea, you'll begin to understand why cruising is the ultimate holiday experience . . . From the moment you step aboard, you'll find a world of choices you could only have imagined. There's a wealth of on board activities available to you day and night, as well as some of the most mouthwatering cuisine, the finest wines, superb on board entertainment and a quality of service you'll find second to none . . . Relive the spirit of fine traditional cruising in true European style, where from the moment you set foot on board you're welcome as somebody special, part of an intimate family . . . Relax and enjoy constant attention that recalls to mind a more gracious era when service reigned supreme . . .'

The glossy brochure is very alluring. It tempts you to steer a vacational trip between the peaceful doldrums of relaxation and the high seas of adventure. The luxury cruise has become the password for lavish self-indulgence. Its promoter would laugh to scorn the opinion of the Roman poet, Horace, that 'they change their climate not their souls who rush across the seas.' Its steam-based history began in 1871 with the launching of the White Star ship, *Oceanic,* the first express luxury liner, a venture that initiated a highly competitive era, especially in terms of the quest for the 'blue riband' for the record voyage across the Atlantic. In 1932 the *Normandie*, 1000ft long and carrying 2000 passengers, ushered in the modern liners, and then, to gladden British hearts, the *Queen Mary* took to the waves. It was the first liner to exceed 1000ft in length and it weighed a colossal 82,000 tons.

Entertainment was from the first one of the ingredients. The White Star had poached W H Hartley, the *Mauritania* bandmaster, to conduct the *Titanic* orchestra, with 253 songs in the file that had to be perfectly known, along with pianist Theodore Brailey and cellist Roger Bricoux from the *Carpathia*. A modest plaque in the Liverpool Philharmonic Hall records their bravery, and that of their colleagues, bass-violinist Fred Clark and violinist Jock Hume, neither of whom had shipped before, and others, whose music tried to comfort and calm the stricken passengers on that tragic April night in 1912. At the last they played, not *Nearer to Thee, My God, This Night,* as some rumours had it, but the Episcopal hymn, *Autumn.* More happily, it was Henry Hall, who, having replaced Jack Payne as the BBC resident dance band leader two years previously, led his orchestra on the *Queen Mary's* maiden voyage.

By the 1970s the cruise experience had become rather more demotic. As air travel extended and cheapened, it encompassed the notion of a flight to the Mediterranean or the Caribbean to embark on a holiday voyage, with boats conveying from 500 to 2000 passengers through such maritime delights. By the last quarter of the 20th century, tourism, it was claimed, was 'Europe's largest industry', accounting for 6% of the European Community's Gross National Product, 6% of its capital investment and a tenth of its labour force. Each year 100 million Europeans take

200 million holidays, 30% of them involving air travel. A proportion of these were engaged on cruises. Entertainment followed the mercantile flag. The flight to the Costa Brava had started to dent the customary British seaside holiday trade and, with it, the livelihood of many entertainers. Some resorts depended more on day trippers, ferried thither in the ubiquitous car, while there was also a movement away from the big theatre productions to more small-scale cabaret in night clubs. Of course, some places – Blackpool, Great Yarmouth, for instance – continued to support quality light theatre, but there was some decline in the kind of holiday show-business in which John Wade had somewhat specialised. Naturally enough, there was not an undue demand, although there was some, for British acts on the continent.

The cruise ship was different. The cruise ship is a peripatetic seaside resort of the classier sort. It is St Tropez in aquatic motion. Such being the case, the demand for the fleshpots is exorbitant, covering a glamorous range of gaming, swimming, banqueting and, of course, performing. John Wade was ideally prepared and ready for the cruising fray. He had made his mainline theatrical debut in the West End. He emulated that distinction by jumping into the cruise market at its deep end. The Bernard Delfont agency booked him for the *Queen Elizabeth II,* monarch of the seas. Such was its modish opulence that the *QE2* embraced its 2000 passengers so lovingly that its supporting cast of crew and assorted stewards, chefs, hairdressers and entertainers totalled almost as many again, so that 4000 sailed on the good ship. In cricketing parlance, there were as many Players as Gentlemen; it was what Sir Alf Ramsey, the late England football manager, might have termed 'man for man marking.'

John Wade first sailed in 1972, just a year or two into the liner's regal life, with the luxury concept still in its first flush. A first-class cabin was then *de riguer* for artists, who were treated with immense respect. John was paid a full week's money –

a magnanimous £250 – for the five day trip, without the anxieties of having to find lodgings in the backstreet of a northern mill-town. Later there would be the harder times. An entertainer might be asked to take a cut in fees, in exchange for a free ride for his or her spouse, while extra tasks might be insisted on, like comedians calling the bingo numbers or dancers acting as hostesses at the captain's parties. In those early days, however, it was luxurious. Over the two or three years during which John offered magic to the Transatlantic voyagers, he could sing, with the crew of *HMS Pinafore,* 'we sail the ocean blue and our saucy ship's a beauty'.

John Wade proceeded to crisscross the Atlantic 22 times, (11 passages there and 11 back), with a 36 hour stopover each time in New York. British war movies were once curtly apostrophised as John Mills keeping a stiff upper lip on the bridge while Richard Attenborough had hysterics in the engine room. Something of that same dichotomy applied to entertainment on the *QE2*. There was a huge ballroom-cum-theatre and a smaller compact chamber. Joe Loss and his band, doubtless signing on with the happy rhythms of *In the Mood*, played for the dancers in the bigger arena and proffered backing to the singing stars, such as Dick Haymes or Donald O'Connor. At the same time, John Wade, conjuring, compering, conversing, would play host, a musical trio at his beck and call, to the party-goers in the smaller room. The second night out, the roles would be reversed, with John taking over in the more spacious setting; they would alternate again on the next two nights, before forces were joined for combined operations on the final evening before landfall.

Cruise voyagers, like seaside promenaders, are anticipating enjoyment, seeking to find pleasure in their nautical surrounds, provided it has the requisite taste of extravagance. The work was certainly demanding, but it was not unpleasant and it had its quota of fascination. The courtly liner is a floating statelet. Everyone soon knows everyone who is anyone. Its entertainers are as instantaneously recognisable as TV soaps stars or high-ranking royals. Once John slipped into the lounge bar for a reviving drink and a fellow-passenger spotted him and joined him for some serious dialogue. It was Frank Capra. Once, around midnight, John was on deck, leaning on the handrail, contemplating life and the Atlantic, when he was approached by someone who had enjoyed his act and wished to engage him in quiet converse for some minutes. It was Billy Graham.

Turning the candle at both ends .... John Wade makes light of his bewitching work

Such abundance . . . and then came the crisis. John Wade would be embarrassed were his chief professional trauma to be written up in terms of Greek tragedy. Nonetheless, there was something of hubris in the manner of its unfolding. It struck at the moment of his highest achievement and some at least of the seeds of his severest challenge were sown in the very attainment of his success. John Wade had, for some years, been leaping from peak to peak in career terms, like a mountain goat crossing the Andes. It could scarcely be improved upon, with his success perhaps beyond anything he had dreamed of in those days, 20 years before, when an invitation to do ten minutes in a church hall had been like an urgent call to top the bill at the Palladium.

Poignantly, therefore, it was on one of his *QE2* cruises that the first intimations of his wretched ailment were visited upon him. Even more poignantly, he was actually swimming in one of the ship's grandiose pools, gleaming emblem of this opulent lifestyle, when the ship's doctor remarked a physical curio. He spotted that John was swimming crookedly, favouring his port rather than his starboard side, almost to the point of swimming in circles. He then also noted that John, when carrying his equipment, would switch it from one hand to the other whenever he came to a door that needed a considerable push to open it. These were material cues of which John himself was hardly aware. The doctor, utilising the full range of the facilities in his high-class on board clinic, treated him with massage and advised him to seek specialist advice when next on *terra firma.*

It was arthritis. Moreover, it was arthritis of, *inter alia,* the wrists and hands. If the footballer dreads the creaking knee, the trumpeter the lost *embouchure*, the pianist the dulled ear or the painter the weakened eye, what more fell complaint can assail the magician than crippled fingers?

It was the beginning of a personal and physical nightmare, for, later, John Wade was to suffer abysmal spinal problems. Furthermore, there is strong evidence to suggest that a part of the cause was unwittingly self-induced by the exigencies of his profession. Tales abound of how crafts mar their distinguished exponents, such as inventors who suffer fatally because of their creation. Poor James Brindley, who constructed the Bridgewater Canal in 1759, Britain's first major artificial waterway, who went on to map 360 miles of canal and who, although an illiterate who never committed a calculation to paper, founded, with John Smeaton, the British school of civil engineering, is reputed to be such an example. He fell in one of his blessed canals. So miserly was his pittance from his patron, the Duke of Bridgewater, that he had never been able to afford a change of clothes. As a result, salvaged from the cold waterway, he struggled on shivering in soaked garb, caught pneumonia and died in 1772.

The Bridgewater Canal, despite John's current biographer having been bred alongside its banks, is small beer compared with the Atlantic and trips on *Queen Elizabeth II*, and the consequences for John were, luckily, not as lethal. But it does seem those early years of, night after and night, carting and carrying two weighty cases of magical equipment, on and off trains and buses, up stairs and down stairs, along countless miles of roadway to the distant outposts of urban conviviality, had weakened the joints. While John Wade was now being paid handsomely for his youthful determination and ambition, another price was being levied in cruel pain and the threat of professional disaster. The plot, like the perfidious joint, thickened.

With pure artistic integrity, John Wade chose to suffer this calamity at the very juncture when the United Kingdom, indeed, the western world, was undergoing its first principal economic upheaval of the post-war period. The oil crisis of 1973/74, when fuel prices quadrupled, threw the world into turmoil and triggered a long-standing global recession that, in spite of a debt-led rally in the early 1980s, bit deep into the 1990s. Where for a score of years the British economy had grown at an average annual rate of 3%, now 1% was considered something of a bonus. The danger signal of inflation indicated that, using a base of 100 in 1962, the index had passed 500 by 1982 and 1000 by 1992 – John Wade's £250 a week suddenly appeared less rosy. Full employment, complacently taken for granted since 1940, collapsed and, by the late 1970s, unemployment had surged to three millions.

The complement to these economic hazards was a sense of disillusion with the so-called Butskellite post-war consensus, named after the Tory elder statesman, Rab Butler, and the Labour politician, Hugh Gaitskell. This was based on Keynesian economics, fiscally stimulating demand in bad times and quietening it in good, coupled with strongly subsidised public services and amenities. These civil practices, from schools to hospitals, from gas and electricity companies to telephones and buses, now looked austere, outmoded, anonymous, incompetent, abrasive and officious. The mentality of the soup kitchen frequently prevailed in such provision, whereas Sainsburys and the other supermarkets offered a more fashionable image to the consumer. There was an additional and intangible element. Aneurin Bevan, ebullient creator of the National Health Service, was wont to remark that societies, imperceptibly and without reason, swung on a pendulum between being dog-like, all cheerful and co-operative, and cat-like, all fiercely independent and selfish. This was definitely a feline clime. The social unity of the 1940s, with its faith in planned public endeavour and civic virtue, had gradually yielded to a much more individualistic sentiment. It was to be closely identified with Margaret Thatcher, although most commentators would now agree that she rode rather than created the mood.

Privatism, in personal dealings and in the overall fabric of the state, in respect, for instance, of unfettered marketing and the commercialisation of hitherto public undertakings, became paramount. As often paradoxically happens with free enterprise responses in the economic field, there was, in alliance, an eager belief in central discipline and nationalistic fervour in the cultural and social arenas. Local authorities, for example, were shorn of power, while services that had enjoyed some communal components, like policing or the school curriculum, were remorselessly controlled from the centre. Moreover, almost all the social indices were depressingly negative. It is not easy to extricate cause and effect from among the complex social factors, but there was a desperate upsurge of poverty, of crime, of socially constructed disease (for example through drug and alcohol abuse) and of what the criminologists call 'incivilities', illustrated in graffiti, rowdyism and vandalism. The yearly criminal offences in the 1940s totalled, on average, less than half a million, whereas, by the late 1970s, it was well over two millions; the sum of violent crimes quadrupled in the same period.

Inevitably, this shift in national consciousness and organisation was to leave its mark on the entertainment industry, as we shall note in regard of John Wade's career, over the next 20 years. The luxury cruise, incidentally, was one portent of these changes, for it catered for a particular fairly high income range, whereas, traditionally, other conduits of entertainment, like the variety theatre, with its stalls and gallery, or the seaside resort, with its more 'select' and cheaper ends of the 'front', had tended to offer the same product to all classes at a price differential. Remember the quotation from the cruises brochure at the head of this chapter: the passengers are invited to enjoy an experience that 'recalls to mind a more gracious era.' It amounted to the slight widening of what overwhelmingly had been an upper class preserve, rather than a general post, *à la* the Spanish beaches and islands, for almost everyone to join in at some level.

Be that as it may, here was John Wade, with his country slumping and his bones aching. So what did John do in this the hour of a national recession he scarcely yet associated with his own pressing physical problems?

Arthritis is a cruel fate. Browse through one of those terrifying but irresistible medical books that appear to dwell in every lay household. Tome-like becomes tomb-like, as the cringing patient magnifies a mere sniffle into terminal disease of unutterable agony and curses his or her overzealously enquiring mind. Arthritis arrives belatedly at page 474 of our household dictionary of death.

We learn that, strictly speaking, the term should only be applied to the inflammation of joints and their surrounding structures, but that both doctors and patients have adopted it as a sometimes misleading blanket epithet for a wide range of rheumatoid disorders. There is much else. Suffice it to say that the inflammatory process, the fundamental cause of which is hardly understood, affects the soft tissues of the lining of the joint and may lead to an excess of the fluid that lubricates the joint. Swelling and stiffness result. Such degenerative activity occurs in many people, indeed is almost universal as a fact of wear and tear. It is, needless to say, the degree of intensity that is critical. John Wade tells the sad tale of helping with a tree-planting function for one of the arthritis charities which he has so generously helped over the years. One of his arboreal colleagues was a 14 year old schoolgirl, a fellow-sufferer. She was dead within the year.

John Wade's doctor, approached after the alarm bells sounded on that last cruise, offered peremptory and no-nonsense advice, rather after the manner of a Victorian headmaster: 'learn to live with it.' The prognosis was appalling. John's arthritis had adopted the old regimental motto, *ubique* – it was everywhere. It even had its own prefix. It was Polyarthritis. It struck with regular nastiness in the knees, lingered awhile, then switched to the shoulders, and so on in a ghastly game of now-you-feel-me-now-you-don't, an unwelcome visitor, turning up unexpectedly in different parts of the bone structure, but always to be discovered somewhere. Barely in his 40s, and fearful not only for his hard-won professional laurels but for his very lifestyle, the grinding cogs of the wheelchair were on the not too distant horizon.

John Wade turned to his multi-talented friends in the Savage Club for guidance and, in particular, to his fellow-member, David Hughes. David Hughes agreed that John had to learn to live with it, but emphasised that, as in all learning, the quality of the lessons was the vital component. An amiable, gentle figure of a medical man, almost prim in the composed precision of his care and attention, the key to the learning regimen was to be his watchful monitoring, whether it was of physical or medicinal aids.

David Hughes took untold care with his guardianship of John's complaint. There were neck braces and wrist cuffs of foam rubber and there were hot wax treatments for the hands. The painkilling drugs were tried and tested in an attempt to find the optimal cocktail. John Wade embarked on a daily dosage of 12 to 15 tablets – the same John who, as a child, had steadfastly refused his mother's abjuration to take even an aspirin. They included the ones that dampened the agony substantially but caused the pavements to sway like a gale-swept suspension bridge, hardly the right recipe for an entertainer driving a thousand miles a week. Slowly, some kind of compromise was reached between the excruciating ache and an analgesic programme that was not so overwhelming as to rule out normalcy of work and play. It is a shifting and fragile balance, one that John has already lived with these 30 years.

Worse followed. The arthritis in his wrists stemmed the flow along the nerve cables to his fingers, so that there was perpetually stinging pins and needles, day and night, and a frightening numbness. John Wade found himself performing tricks and not being able to feel the articles he was holding. He did his act at two nightclubs without really knowing whether or not he was grasping his props. There were moments when it looked as if the bright career was to be terminated just as it had begun to glow resplendently. John's workload had just reached the comforting point where, rather than wondering what might turn up next week, he was being engaged six and 12 months ahead, with a list of bookers to ring whenever gaps appeared in the schedule. Sleeplessness had a dual cause: the physical discomfort and the mental anguish.

There was a further Savage intervention. David Hughes referred John to Basil Helal, than whom there was no more distinguished name in the orthopaedic field. To relieve the condition, Basil Helal twice deployed hydrocortisone shots, where the exactitude of that miniaturist embroidery is essential. One time it was the clinical equivalent of a bull's eye and relief ensued for a time; the other time was not quite so successful, such was the pinpoint accuracy required. The decision was made to operate at the Royal London Hospital.

Basil Helal determined on the bilateral carpel tunnel syndrome operation. For those readers whose surgical knowledge has perhaps grown a little rusty, it might be explained that this involved opening the duct in the wrist through which ran the nerves to the hands and digits. Then the arthritic debris, which hindered the nerve messages *en route* to the fingers, was cleansed away and the passage left open in the hope that there would be no reoccurrence of the blockage. In the terminology of underground railway construction, what was once a tunnel became a cut-and-cover tube.

John Wade sat demurely in his hospital cot, as Basil Helal arrived, accompanied by medical students, pale and wanly loitering. A kindly but tall and imposing figure, Basil Helal, with his intelligent eye and cerebral brow, had something of the aura that those of us who rely on telly's medical soaps for our prototypes would associate with a real-life consultant. The students, equal in their subscription to stereotyping, were understandably loath to ask questions of or proffer answers to their respected supremo. In a cameo that might have been borrowed from the 1954 farce, *Doctor in the House,* starring James Robertson Justice in the Basil Helal role and Dirk Bogarde and Kenneth More among the L-plated pupils, the consultant authoritatively announced his intention to perform the bilateral carpel tunnel syndrome operation, that is, with both wrists treated at the same time.

It was customary, where both hands were involved, to undertake the two invasive procedures at a six weeks interval, so that the patient had one effective hand throughout. Now it was time to go bilateral, but the students were nonplussed when asked what the reason might be for this break with convention. Basil Helal suggested that they ask Mr Wade what his occupation was. They obliged and John, somewhat ingenuously, told them he was an entertainer. Silence pursued its sombre reign. The consultant prompted them to inquire as to what sort of entertainer Mr Wade might be. The students sought this further information. Ah ! A magician: comprehension dawned. Basil Helal explained that the calls for a one-handed magician were rare and that six weeks unemployment for a professional conjuror was disastrous enough, let alone 12 weeks. It was an excellent lesson in holistic medicine.

There was a social lesson as well. This was all done courtesy of the dear old National Health Service, without a penny-piece for the commercial sector. It was a standing tribute to the civic virtue of a redoubtable public service, which, on its occasional better days, merits the compliment paid to it by the American political commentator, A L Lindsay, that the NHS is 'one of the great achievements of the 20th century', not least in that it was, in the words of Rudolf Klein, one of its most expert analysts, 'the first health system in any Western society to offer free medical care to the entire population.'

What is undeniable is that John Wade profited immensely from those who shepherded and steered him through the labyrinthine system. His case is a potted version of the research during the 1960s that demonstrated that uniform social provision is susceptible to the range of know-how and energetic persistence of the clientele. It was found, for example, that, in the NHS, for every £124 spent on the health care of a professional person, only £88 was expended on a semi-skilled or unskilled worker, just as, in state schools, for every £90 spent on the child of a professional family, only £60 was spent on the child of a semi-skilled or unskilled worker's family. Basically, the middle classes showed more wit and persistence in making the public services operate at maximum efficacy. The ethical concern is not that John Wade cajoled the system in doing what it was supposed to do with brisk efficiency, but that, without that kind of informed massage, it sometimes lets down others less capable of discovering the most effective routeways.

For all that good fortune, the professional price was heavy. John Wade had been, as a result of his televisual notoriety, rewarded with a prestigious booking on the Bailey circuit, with dates in the nation's top-line clubs, like the bustling Golden Garter, Wythenshawe, Greater Manchester. These were examples of another twist in the rarely still yarn of show-business. Some of the working men's clubs of old, usually based on the compact foundation of a manufacturing unit, such as a colliery or a mill, had, in the consumer boom of the late 1950s and 1960s, become commercialised and developed a gaudy taste for national and international celebrity entertainers. Bernard Manning's Embassy Club in Manchester is a typical illustration. In one sense, this was a substitute for the now-dead variety theatre, but it was something more. With food and, more particularly, drink on offer, and maybe some gambling, it brought to the mass of working class people a glimmer of the exotic nightlife that the metropolitan sophisticates had long enjoyed. It paralleled the Costa Brava experience as an analogue of the old-style upper class vacation in Monte Carlo. It was an exceptionally eminent booking, but a combative one, with the atmosphere sometimes fraught with a sexual and alcoholic tension, so much so that Ken Dodd, ever the alertest of social psychologists when it comes to comedy, has spoken of the need to tell 'release' jokes in such an ambience.

John Wade had begun flourishingly well, but he had been forced to take leave of absence from that lucrative tour, although, later, he did make good the engagements. A disturbing feature was the word was out that John Wade was ill. Few wish to advertise an ailment, but, in show-business, it often pays to hide the dark light of sickness under the bushel of smiling geniality. There is something off-putting about a sick entertainer. Entertainers are supposed to be hale and hearty at all times, just as vicars are expected to be always pious, bank managers ever reliable and undertakers invariably solemn. One or two agents and others tended to cold shoulder John, although, by and large, this was temporary and not widespread. Most associates were sympathetic and helpful. One piece of such good fortune was the offer, following his few days in hospital, of a two weeks cruise across the Mediterranean, right up to the Bosphorus. A friend of John's was the entertainments booker for the Thomson travel agents and he made this gratis offer available, in return for just a couple of conjuring spots during the sail.

Recovery was swift and, given the need to earn, it had to be. Basil Helal, eschewing the mundane slitting of the wrists, had opted for the more spectacular one inch cuts in the palms. While the mechanics of the operation were rendered more difficult, recovery from the procedure was quicker; the tiny wounds healed swiftly and, six months later, John was able to hold up his magicianly hands to the television cameras, knowing that the surgeon would be observing the absence of scarring. John Wade confidently resumed work and, as at other junctures in his variegated career, sought new opportunities.

While the professional chances altered, the medical condition remained grimly constant. Several people have gushingly told John Wade over the last 30 years that he has been courageous in tackling the disease. He would, rightly, refute the notion that he is a brave soldier. On the whole, brave soldiers have an element of choice, with medals going to those whose heroics go beyond the immediate call of duty. John Wade had no choice. Some, according to Malvolio's anonymous letter, have greatness thrust upon them, whereas, for John Wade, it was arthritis. He was stuck with it; eventually, it might wear him down and out. The motivating emotion was sheer funk, although maybe the frontiers of fear and valour mingle. The question for John was whether he could muster the strength of attitude to delay the devils in pursuit of his skeletal frame.

He could and he did. The zest and ambition that drove him as a youth was rekindled in middle age to thwart, however temporarily, the threat to his working and leisure life. Few realise the daily endeavour this necessitates. As well as the daily pills – smaller in number now, because the pharmaceutical chemistry is more sophisticated – and the employment of electrically charged pads for easement, there is another range of tricks for coping, a kind of alternative magicianship. For three decades John has, before doing his turn, usually swallowed a glass of Scotch. Yes, admittedly, there are fouler specifics, but this is an artist who never drank at all for many years and who, before the arthritic calamity, would have looked unkindly on the entertainer who fortified himself with alcohol, so frequently the cause of the downfall – Sid Field; Tony Hancock – of great performers. John Wade found, and he quotes medical chapter and verse, that the Caledonian libation would halt the pain for 15 minutes, just sufficiently to manipulate the thimbles, the vanishing mirror and the invisible pack of cards. He also uses an analgesic spray, of the brand witnessed by fans being applied to writhing football stars, on his hands and fingers. It penetrates the skin quickly and, just for ten minutes or so, gives enough relief for the show to go on.

Some things changed. John Wade had become a desultory golfer. It was his habit, along with a fellow nightclub entertainer, to arrive home about three in the morning, nap for a couple of hours, present himself at the first tee of the Richmond municipal course at about eight o'clock, hook and slice fiercely over a few holes – and then return home and climb up the dancers to Bedfordshire again. Any illusions this illusionist had (to be just, they were negligible) about a deception that exchanged a Maskelyne for a Jacklin had to be permanently shelved. Otherwise he, for the main part, soldiered on. Looking a little ahead in the interests of coherence of biographical material, he was assessed as 'disabled' in 1983 and obtained the coveted parking badge. In another slant on progressive social policy, what impressed the assessors was John's refusal to buckle. It was his patent desire to continue working, and his practical requirement to drive straight up to stage doors to unload his heavy gear, that told. Of course, he knows that, ultimately, Queen Polyarthritis will rule supreme. He counts the times he struggles on the stairway of his local station, as he journeys back and forth to his beloved Savage Club, well aware that, some day, even that beneficent pleasure may be denied or, at least, require a less attractive variant for its accomplishment.

Another curio was that, after the onset of his illness, John Wade never designed a new trick for himself. The psychology is fascinating. A quarter of a century of ingrained and habitual practice of a tranche of tricks withstood the malign instructions of afflicted bones. Woe betide John did he attempt some novelty or even if he practised some older artifice. As soon as he started consciously thinking about the processes, the arthritis crashed through the threshold of stubborn routine and he foundered. One is reminded of the Guy de Maupassant story of the professional knife-thrower, who decided to kill his unfaithful wife. For years she had been his human target, around whom he pitched blades, just missing her, so that, he surmised, an accidental death could easily be fabricated. Come the homicidal attempt, and he discovered that the implanted usage could not be overridden. He could not hit her fair and square, but persisted in drilling the customary pattern around his terrified wife and partner. A little less epically, part of the John Wade rapprochement with his dire complaint was the inability to undertake new tricks and the inability to stop performing old ones.

Another significant factor was the accumulation of gadgets. John Wade surrounded himself with an ever-expanding legion of mechanical contraptions. Tap levers; light-handled knives; a tool for picking up stuff from the floor that an old-fashioned park-keeper would have killed for, and a hundred other technical devices. Where have we heard something like this before? We remember the eager fuse-mending, Meccano-splicing, aeroplane-modelling, trick-manufacturing schoolboy, the busy boy scout, with a shirt-arm blazoned with proficiency badges and a penknife with an attachment for taking drawing pins out of the padded feet of hippopotami or whatever.

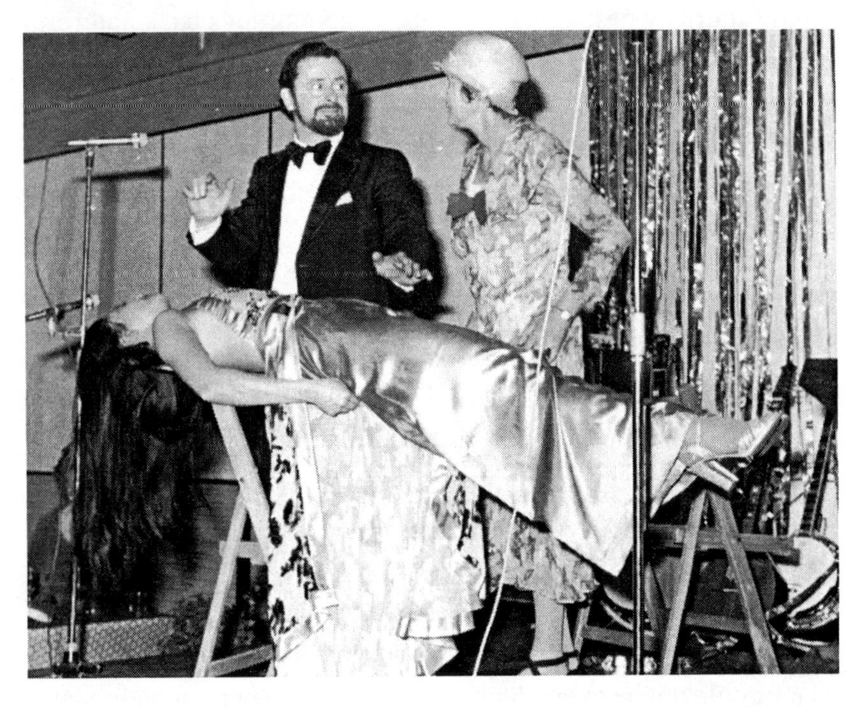

An uplifting moment . . . Pat Coombs joins John Wade as he levitates Wei Wei Wong for a charity event

When in trouble, make or do something overtly practical and, if possible, technically adept and staggeringly ingenious. When home and school had menaced him and placed him in peril of mental suffocation, he liberated himself, in part, through gadgetry. Faced with the crisis of illness, his grinning joy in inventions was to come again to his aid. Of course, they do work and assist in actuality, but, overall, this is more about a man escaping from the bondage of sickness via a freeing pleasure in technology. It is his method of coping, or, as magicians would say, of distraction. Some would find solace in improving literature or advertising for a volunteer carer or prayer or getting drunk or writing their autobiography or turning their face to the wall while the arthritis trots by.

Not John Wade. Faithful to the energetic dictates of his inherent character, he found salvation once more in a schoolboy's delight in gadgets. The spirit of William Brown, inquisitive, opportunist, experimenting, now walked, albeit a little stiffly, the streets of London W4. What a Godsend John Wade would have been to the inmates of Colditz! Come to think of it, there in Colditz was a whole bunch of men intent on inventing and producing all manner of hare-brained artefacts, of an assortment they might have read about in the *Hotspur* or *Wizard* comics of their boyhood, certainly directed at escape, but, as several recognised, also as a mode of managing the stress of the problem. Outwitting German guards and outwitting serious incapacity may have a common denominator.

John Wade commenced the remoulding of his imperilled career while in hospital. He became an author. An editor who had heard John discussing magic on the Pete Murray radio programme had asked him to consider committing the material to book form and now he agreed. Robert Harbin, that resplendent and highly inventive wizard, consented to be interviewed at the Wade hospital bedside and work was soon underway. *The Trade of the Tricks; Magic, Magicians and the Magic Circle* was published in 1974 midst many plaudits, including a launch at the Magic Circle headquarters and a double column review by Alan Brien in the *Sunday Times.*

It remains perhaps the most accessible text available on the evolution of the magic arts, from the burial chamber in Beni Hassan, with the cups and balls trick painted on the wall, to Tommy Cooper, with special reference to the history of The Magic Circle and with a breezy thread of autobiographical reference throughout. It also includes a calm explanation, at a time when he was all the rage, of how Uri Geller deploys a brilliant line in misdirection but has introduced no new phenomenon into professional magicianship. Uri Geller has modestly refused to be tested by other conjurors, and, as John Wade suggests, his act raises 'one delicate point of ethics'. By identifying himself as a 'psychic' and by inferring that his powers are uncanny, he may have allowed gullible folk to believe that some supernatural influence is operating. Indeed, this may give him an extra defence, for, as with the charlatan spiritualist medium, watchers may be anxiously seeking for it to happen, whereas, with genuine magicians, spectators are trying to see 'how he did it.' This paragraph is confidently written by a biographer who supports Manchester United and who notes that Reading football club, to whom Uri Geller offered his psychic support, currently languishes at ninth place in the second division (that is, the old third division) of the Football League.

The book was a critical success, an author's euphemism for impoverished repute, but it was another avenue. Soon afterwards John Wade was asked to write a booklet on how to compere, a task for which he was wonderfully well experienced. *Do Get the Name Right* has been reprinted on several occasions and is still doing its helpfully engaging rounds, with many admiring endorsements from celebrities. Moreover, just as *The Trade of the Tricks* had stemmed from media interest, so did it, in turn, lead to more television and radio work.

Pete Murray had used his radio show to wish John Wade good luck for his hospital visitation, which led to a stream of cards from well-wishers decorating his hospital locker. Soon after his convalescence, John was back on *Open House*, rewarding its kindly host by sawing him in half on radio, with the listeners all but hearing

Pete Murray turn pale as John Wade explained it was the first time he had tried the trick. This was part of a special programme produced at the London Palladium with a live audience. There was also a marvellous fusing of the radio and cruise elements when John, with a telephone in his *QEII* cabin and a satellite link, unfolded a mystery whereby a guest in the London studio chose a card of the same denomination as one reversed in a pack and locked in the ship's safe before leaving Southampton.

Television figured very substantially in John Wade's life at this time, and, although a tense and strenuous business, it was probably not as physically sapping as the ceaseless trailing from hotel to club and theatre to nightspot of previous years. Before and during this period John Wade became consultant to and occasional performer on the popular David Nixon series. Balding, mild-mannered, unfailingly courteous, David Nixon, somehow finding a bridge between the chirpy conjuror and the mute wizard, hugged the television set with a gentle assurance. His style was ideal for families ranged on their sofas and armchairs, and, through the 1970s, his sedate presence was welcomed in millions of living-rooms.

The show ended with a big illusion, often incorporating the guest star David Nixon had earlier interviewed and charmed with a close-up trick. Rotund Stubby Kaye, disguised as Santa Claus, turned out to be the plump pianist, Mrs Mills, for one Christmas show, while Stubby Kaye was revealed tied up in a sack of toys. On another programme, plaintive Norman Wisdom, thrust protesting into a dustbin with David Nixon sitting upon it, arrived driving the dustcart intended to empty the container. Anita Harris, frequently on the show, warbling ditties like *Fly me to the moon*, still jokingly reproaches John when they meet about the indignities she suffered as a magical stooge. Cheerfully effusive, she even submitted to driving a motor bike, fulsomely clad in the then trendy hot-pants, and vanishing into thin air.

Oddly enough, TV, for all its millions of viewers inches away from the screen, was the only exception to John Wade's new rule about not doing novel tricks. David Nixon used to start his programme with a smallscale hand-held ruse, and he often failed to think about it even until after the final rehearsal, relying on his magical adviser to dream up some device. This coolness under fire encouraged John himself, on rare occasion, to follow suit. 'Just do it', the adviser was advised by David Nixon, and he just did it. The man who always insists that budding magicians should practise until they drop found that, in his arthritic situation, the only answer, now and then, was the unrehearsed attempt with absolute dependency on unconsciously assimilated skills, a further ramification of the telling potency of inherent disposition.

Televisual trickery . . . the well-liked impressionist, Faith Brown, with John Wade in the TV show *For My Next Trick*

Publication of *The Trade of the Tricks* led directly to a set of appearances on *Pebble Mill at One*, broadcast from the Birmingham-based television studios and on the Thames Television item, *Five Magic Moments,* which went out for five minutes just before five o'clock in the afternoon, allowing time for one trick only. In the mid-1970s John Wade was travelling to 'Jollywood', the old Dickenson Road television studios in Rusholme, Manchester, to film *For My Next Trick.* It was the conjuror's equivalent of Granada's *Comedians*, a quick-fire programme that show-cased a number of comics, like Ken Goodwin, Bernard Manning and Mike Reid, switching rapidly from one to the other. Along with his long-term pals, Terry Seabrooke, and Paul Daniels, John Wade was one of the regulars on *For My Next Trick*, with its mixture of single tricks and magical sketches.

Colour was now *de riguer.* It meant the increased heat of the lighting, a ban on white shirts which appeared a grubby yellow on screen and a rash of urban folk-myths about the intense lighting making false teeth transparent, a rumour that led to some tight-lipped smiles among the acting fraternity. But it also meant bright, clear screens offering lengthy hours of television on several channels in something like 99% of British households. Magicians found a ready stint with the advertisers, for what retailer does not want to claim for his product magical powers? Either fair of face or hands only, there was a point in the 1970s when John Wade was in no less than 13 commercials at the same time, some of them appearing three or four times each evening, and ranging from magical stuff to pour down your throat to magical stuff to rub on your windows.

The degree of coverage was immense and John Wade discovered, in minor part, that which he had noted among the likes of George Harrison and Paul Newman when hob-nobbing with them on the *Queen Elizabeth II.* He was recognised in the street. Once there was a slight mobbing by schoolchildren at the local shops. He was hailed by passers-by and stopped for his autograph. Possibly most telling of all, his dustman started to cry 'Hello John' when he arrived to remove the rubbish, for, whatever his other civic virtues, the yeoman refuse-collector is not ordinarily *au fait* with his clients' appellations, much as he might otherwise identify them by their failure to tie up their plastic bags properly or to ensure that yesterday's casserole remnants do not slop out over his boots.

One evening John Wade, forsaking the car, the tiresomeness of the painful drive and the exhausting search for a parking place within a day's march of the venue, booked a cab for a trip to Poplar. He climbed in the car and off drove the cabby. John gave him the address. The taxi-driver cocked his ear. 'Say something else', he urged. John spoke casually of the state of the weather. 'I know who you are,' cried the chauffeur exultantly, 'you're the idiot that does tricks on the wireless.'

Thus the 1970s wore on, with John Wade thriving, his personal crisis, if not overcome, then at least mastered. There was an evident maturity in his *persona.* For example, he made a heartening re-entry into the wonderful world of pantomime. It would have been so miserably wasteful – a loss to John and a loss to audiences – if he had not obliterated the painful memory of his tenderfoot panto weeks in long-ago Chester and proved to himself that he, a veritable custodian of that cheery verve which is the quintessence of the festive Christmas pantomime, could not fulfil that call. John Wade, a published historian of the Magic Circle, an ardent collector of ancient magicians' posters and memorabilia and a devout keeper of the innate memory of entertainment, could not but succeed in this, the most traditional of its several modes.

In 1974 he enjoyed a splendid success as Baron Hardup in a six weeks run of *Cinderella* at the Civic Theatre, Darlington. Top billing went to the pop group Second Generation, proof that panto is adept at utilising modern manifestations as blood transfusions for its aged carcass. Pantomime has, like Charles II, been 'a long time a-dying', constantly finding tonics, first in music hall stars, then in variety stars, then in radio stars, and finally in television pop and soap stars. Long may it continue to benefit from that continually changing stream of human adrenaline and defy the thousand show-biz counterparts of medical practitioners who have pronounced the patient dead or dying.

Genius of the lamp . . . John Wade stars in *Aladdin* as Abanazar, the magician's dream panto role

Two years later John Wade landed a prestige engagement at the Sunderland Empire, one of Britain's leading panto bookings. It was a two month run and it was *Aladdin*. Peter Goodwright, a fellow-Savage and light comedian with a flavour of George Formby's guileless appeal, was Wishee Washee and Don Smoothey, a versatile survivor of *Stars in Battledress*, Ralph Reader gang-shows and a dozen other outlets for his friendly talents, was Widow Twankey. This left the role of Abanazar to John Wade. With its canvas of oriental mystique, charmed lamp, servile genie and enchanted cave, *Aladdin* is the perfect panto for magic and Abanazar is the perfect part for magicians. John seized the chance with relish and excelled in a welter of eastern roguery that some-how never quite lost him, for all his bristling villainy, the sympathy of the Wearside audiences.

There was also that enjoyable outing which then seemed to be a fixture with the big city pantomime. Between matinee and evening performance on one of the Saturdays of the run, it was off, in cos-tume, to the local fire station, where the firemen and women had organised a Christmas treat for the needy children of the neigh-bourhood and the panto stars were glad to offer talented help. A compound of relishable grub and fire engines, with Abanazar and Princess Balroubadour for afters, is ideal for children and a fine example of joint community enterprise.

Professional opportunities continued to pop up in pleasing array. There was a very different kind of chance at the Christmas of 1977 when he was invited to play the lead in the British premiere of *The Magic Man* at the Mayfair Theatre, London. It ran for six weeks over the Yuletide and new year period and was produced by Peter Cotes, yet another Brother Savage. Described precisely by Eileen Atkins as 'a passionate man of the theatre' and with, among a host of distinctive achievements, a somewhat controversial involvement with the enduring maintenance of *The Mouse Trap,* Peter Cotes loved cricket, criminology, atheism and a dozen other subjects as burningly as he did the stage – and now his attention was fixed on making John Wade a musical star.

The Magic Man had had its world opening in the United States as an introductory vehicle for the youthful illusionist, David Copperfield, young, lithe and beautiful. The English coequal, middle-aged, craggy and crippled with arthritis, rose to the occasion, even if, to sustain the vehicular metaphor, the sleek American racing model was replaced with a battered English vintage saloon. The plot was thin. Illusionist meets girl; illusionist loses girl; illusionist recovers girl. Peter Cotes ensured that John Wade ended up with the heroine, played by the singer, Greta Gouriet, in his arms without him being overloaded with too much singing. What John truly revelled in was that, for the only time in his professional career, the story-line allowed him to present six huge illusions – 'the big boxes' – at each performance. Thus did *The Magic Man* enjoy an unpretentious success in the West End.

Sword-play . . . John Wade in the title role of *The Magic Man*, the stage musical, produced by fellow-Savage, Peter Cotes, Suzette St Clair on the left, while, on the right, is Trudie Styler, now Mrs Sting.

Earlier in 1977 John Wade was engaged by Combined Services Entertainments to cheer the troops in Belfast, Cyprus and Germany, while 1978 found him in Kenya, touring with a pro-am golf exhibition, plus entertainment. It was an enthralling visit, although, regretfully, John had to turn down an offer, on grounds of ill-health, of free golf lessons from the legendary Arnold Palmer. For some years Dickie Henderson organised this annual trip to raise funds for a Nairobi children's home for polio victims. There was a week's golf, with punters queuing up to purchase the privilege of partnering the likes of Eric Sykes or Ritchie Benaud, the famous Australian cricketer and commentator. Dickie Henderson usually included a non-golfer or so as a surprise face at the grand cabaret — and John was faced with the unenviable job of performing between John Mills and Jimmy Tarbuck.

In the meanwhile, he helped out by visiting the children's home itself and doing a couple of magic shows there. John Wade borrowed some equipment from a local magician who had gained possession of some of Jasper Maskelyne's props, that famous wizard having died in Kenya. It was an historic and emotional moment for John, his feelings those of the musician invited to play the maestro's own cherished violin or flute.

These sentiments were mixed with other emotions, for the home, some 80 miles along dusty tracks from Nairobi, touched the heartstrings. The children, most of them aged about eight to 14, were in leg irons. The workshop which manufactured and, as the youngsters grew, updated the apparatus was adjacent to the home and was the chief focus for the fund-raising exercise. The Kenyan who could not walk was then normally reduced to beggary and this attempt to make the children employable – some of them eventually in the workshop itself – was laudable. The children were delighted with the magic in the most fundamentalist fashion. Having no experience of television and having seen no other conjuror, they accepted the magic as, so to speak, reality. If a coin vanished, they did not seek explanations as to where it might be. It had vanished.

The wives and sweethearts of the pro-am golfers accompanied John on one of these trips, carrying gifts of balloons and soft drinks. These were much appreciated, although John Wade had to be recruited to teach the children how to use a straw, another new and magical experience for them, while, as the visitors departed, the coloured straws were being decoratively plaited in the girls' hair and the knots of the balloons carefully untied – they were much too precious to risk explosion; much better to fold them neatly and sleep with them under one's pillow.

The full complement of celebrities accompanied John Wade on the other visit and, after his show, there was a football match, the sides captained by Bobby Charlton and Jimmy Tarbuck. An asphalt court and leg irons meant that the sparks were literally flying, as the fearless children engaged in a frenzied and vigorous game of maximum commitment. One child disputed a decision by thumping the referee in the stomach with tiny flailing fists, despite the fact that this official was Henry Cooper, renowned as being one of few heavyweight boxers to have felled Muhammad Ali. John Wade inadvertently arrested this pulsating encounter in its energetic tracks. He had packed up his props and had joined the spectators. He slowly lit his post-show pipe. The game stopped. The children stared in amazement. The furry-faced magic man was igniting himself. Jimmy Tarbuck had to urge John to complete his pyrotechnics so that the game could be resumed.

The whole tour was a salutary reminder, not just of the innocence and the heartening resilience of childhood, but of the responsibility of entertainers, as of other adults, to its sensitivities and needs. John Wade found it personally fulfilling and professionally helpful: a year later in 1979, as a consequence of his success, he was invited back to Kenya to do a month's cabaret at the New Stanley Hotel, Nairobi.

Also in 1979 John Wade had a smash-hit on *The Good Old Days*, that much-loved show which came from the City Varieties, Leeds and which, with its fancy-dressed audience, for which honour there was a waiting list of several years' standing, nostalgically recreated some version of the old-time music hall. John Wade, affably able to form an easygoing relation with practically any audience, swooped on so hospitable a body with sheer relish. Donning his Victorian evening dress, he delighted everyone in what was possibly his finest single moment on television.

Gone was the near-frenzy of the 1960s, with three engagements on many nights, with work every day of the week in every corner of every shire, and with the car clocking up the miles by the several tens of thousand. There had been the crucial motive of ambition: 'Fame is the spur', sang John Milton, 'that the clear spirit doth raise (that last infirmity of noble mind) to scorn delights and live laborious days.' There had been the severe pressure to make money to pay bills and sustain a high standard of suburban living for a growing family. Now some of these stresses were easing; the ambitions had been attained; the income was more assured and the monetary demands did not figure quite so largely.

Compared with the rushing hither and thither of the 1960s, there was now, in relative terms, some repose. Of course, apart from the lowered temperature of domestic and self-engendered coercion, John Wade had to pace himself physically in order to guarantee his professional longevity. Then there was a positive reason. He was paid more. The economic depression that started in the mid-1970s had some strange effects. Although there was less employment, those who had occupation tended to be well-paid. This was one of the chief differences between the 1930s slump and its 1970s/1980s successor. The former was a low-wage, low-price deflationary affair, so that the difference between those in work and on the dole was often marginal. The latter was a high-wage, high-price inflationary affair, so that the same gap was now critically wide. In entertainment, as elsewhere, the established workers, among whom John Wade was properly numbered, earned handsome livings.

For example, the new thirst for corporate functions offered new opportunities for entertainers. The large-scale corporation, all image and logo, was itself something of a new phenomenon. In John Wade's childhood an insurance company might have been represented by a mackintoshed, cadaverous figure, wobbling down the street on a bike, calling at houses, upon whose mantelpieces or sideboards were kept pink or buff insurance cards. The few pence would be handed over and a hieroglyphic would be scribbled on the card – and that was a weekly ritual. Hence the Donald M'Gill-type picture postcard, with the insurance agent, at the door of the terraced house, asking 'is your mother in the Prudential?' and the snotty-nosed infant answering, 'no, she's in the outside lavvy.' There was not much room for a magician in that setup, but now the razzmatazz was such that the Prudential company might, at its awards ceremony at a first-class London hotel, pay John Wade £200 or £300 for 15 minutes of magic.

For all that, one does also sense a slackening of the stress, a feeling that John is now very much more the seasoned professional performer, confident that there will always be some demand for his cards and thimbles and for his engaging knack as a master of ceremonies. To some extent, the 'laborious days' were behind him. Now there might be one engagement a week, where, not long before, there had been 20. There was no need to do the summer show now. In any event, it made more economic sense to seek the one-night bookings with good fees rather than decamp to the seaside, setting up in pricey alternative accommodation and leaving one's own housing unused. John Wade's self-belief, as artist and as human being, that we saw burgeon suddenly some years before, was strengthened, not least through his own conflict, determinedly resolved, with adversity.

Royal Command . . . John Wade is greeted by Prince Charles on the occasion of that glittering gala show at Windsor

In the late 1970s John Wade was one of a stellar galaxy, including Dickie Henderson, most relaxed of light comedians and the most loveable Buttons of his generation, and Arthur Askey, that happy-go-lucky, diminutive purveyor of nonsense songs . . . and Michael Bentine and Harry Worth and Susan Hampshire . . . The stars were asked to shine at the Theatre Royal, Windsor, in a fund-raising show for the spastics charity patronised by the Prince of Wales. John Wade's act went splendidly in that compact and cosy old theatre, packed to the rafters with high paying customers. It approximated to a Royal Command Performance and, for the entertainers, there was the additional prize of a supper of banquet-like proportions at Windsor Castle.

The heir to the throne confided in his magicianly subject-to-be his anxiety that there was 'oodles of food' and his concern that an abundance would be wasted. John gallantly reassured the prince that, whatever the press reports, the incidence of anorexia nervosa among the performing brother- and sisterhood was very much exaggerated. Early the next morning, as the party hummed, a delighted if astonished prince met up again with John Wade: pointing dramatically at the empty tables, he murmured. 'it's all gone.'

The compliment had been reversed: a regal spread of delicious comestibles and soothing liquors in reward for a sovereign repast of sumptuous entertainment. Deservedly among those luminous stars, quipping and duping, had been John Wade, a princely jester of diverting gifts, an appetising dish in a feast fit for a king-to-be.

Chapter Five
THE 1980s
ONLY CONNECT

So John Wade, professionally in top form if physically under par, turned his unfailingly eager countenance to the unkind 1980s. It was not too propitious a decade for entertainers, what with the continued closure of theatres and ever tougher restrictions on drinking and driving. It all contributed to people withdrawing steadily into their homes and gluing their eyes to the telly.

The torrent of crime also drove folk indoors, forcing them to barricade their houses and self-impose a curfew. To be exact, it was – it is – that other reality, the fear of crime, that is the chief culprit. For instance, although young people are six times more likely than old people to be the victims of either burglaries or street offences, older people often suffer grave feelings of danger and unease. Three-fifths of women over 60 in central city areas and two-fifths of women over 60 in other urban districts feel 'very unsafe' on the streets after dark. That generational imbalance was possibly further illustrated by the dominance of popular music and the youth cults of the era. A vibrant musical industry made London the world's 'pop' capital, but it was scarcely the context for the friendly arts of old-style variety.

On the magical front, it was a time when many apprentice conjurors were only able to ply their craft on the very streets which were proving so unpleasant to many pedestrians and shoppers. Street-theatre grew common, with, not without some irony, a Covent Garden booking, extramural rather than operatically intramural, the star billing. It was, of course, a testing business. The young magician had no opportunity to set up the act; it was a matter of arriving, touting for an audience and then building the presentation directly from bag and pockets. The Magic Circle recognised this development by adding a 'best street magician of the year' to its illustrious awards ceremony.

It was, then, an uncomfortable period. There was violence abroad and at home. The Falklands campaign of 1982 evoked xenophobic sentiments, with controversy still raging over whether the sinking of the Argentine battleship, *Belgrano*, was a deliberate ploy to stall a potentially effective Peruvian peace initiative. This Jingoism was also the credo of alcohol-fuelled football hooligans, while racial tension led to outbreaks of calamitous rioting from Toxteth to Tottenham. Despite the fitful mirage of recovery, upheaval in the economic arena brought unemployment on a scale unknown since pre-war years, together with grim levels of relative impoverishment, especially affecting children.

The domestic event that probably marked, indeed, scarred the 1980s was the Miners' Strike of 1984/85. It was a fiercesome clash of extremes, of embattled workers against legitimate government, of old-time labourism *versus* newly proclaimed unfettered market forces, of Arthur Scargill, with a somewhat crude Marxian analysis, and Margaret Thatcher, with a not much more polished version of Americanised free marketeering. Many, conscious of both the licit responsibility of an elected ministry and yet the historic place of the mining industry in British life, watched uneasily, as the struggle was joined. Several ruefully nodded in agreement as Neil Kinnock, then the Labour Party leader, borrowed a telling World War I coinage to describe the miners' predicament: 'lions led by donkeys.'

In that oft recurring paradox in times when politicians press for unrestricted commercial enterprise, the government indulged in a massive programme of heavy centralisation. During the Miners' Strike, for example, as many as 180,000 police personnel were trained and involved in crowd control, with a national centre masterminding the operation. It was the closest the United Kingdom had approximated, since the inauguration of modern policing, to the kind of nationalised '*gens d'armerie*' force of a continental brand that had always been suspect in the more liberal climes of Great Britain. Local government was permanently damaged, many of its powers snatched away into the hands of one or other of the 1400 and more non-elected Quangos that now formed 'the new magistracy'. This left the municipalities responsible for raising less than an eighth of the money required to be spent in their environs, with a corresponding plunge in local control and responsibility.

By and large, these were not the most joyous of times, but, of course, the appetite for entertainment was unflagging, with people seeking escape from the nastiness of a riven society. It is no accident that a comedian like Les Dawson came robustly to the fore in the 1980s. That 'doom-laden dumpling' gave morose voice to the social *angst* of the epoch. He drew of a mordant tradition of resigned northern commentary and owed a particular debt, which he generously acknowledged, to the Fanny Fairbottom of Norman 'Over the Garden Wall' Evans. It was Norman Evans who asked a sick neighbour, 'don't you think you should have your bed moved downstairs? They'll never get a coffin round this landing.'

Les Dawson's was the recession of the 1980s, not the slump of the 1930s. It was the criminal barbarism – 'I was mugged by a nun in

Bootle last night' – of his time and it was the bleak corporation housing estates, not the terraced back-to-backs that drew his lugubrious attention: 'I'm not saying our council estate is a long way out of Manchester, but our rent man's a Norwegian.' There was poverty (his father, unable to afford fuel, frightened the children with ghost stories, so they would huddle together and keep warm, whilst another practice of his was to throw IOUs in the wishing well for luck); there was poor housing, with a council flat so damp that his father, in lieu of bedtime stories, organised lifeboat drill. If holidays were affordable, it was now the discomforts of Spain, rather than the horrors of Morecambe. Robbed of everything by brigands on the Costa Brava, his wife saved the passports and pesetas by stuffing them in her mouth. 'It's a pity we didn't bring your mother', was Les Dawson's laconic rejoinder, 'we could have saved the luggage as well.'

Les Dawson, the man who claims to have shot his parents to go on the orphans' picnic and whose mother-in-law 'had a mouth like a workhouse oven', did not consciously set out to be the standard-bearer of 1980s brutalism. Nor was he, as Karl Marx and Fredrich Engels might have envisioned, part of the cultural 'superstructure' unavoidably determined by the underlying economic 'structure'. The relationship was more complex and subtle than that. It was about the laurels going to the comedian whose tone chimed in most effortlessly with the mood of the hour. *Ecce homo*: cometh the hour; cometh the man; just as Robb Wilton accurately reflected the patient, quietly grumbling temper of war-time Britain or Tony Hancock, outwardly braggart, inwardly nerve-wracked, was a precise lightning conductor for the 1950s, doleful Les Dawson spoke grittily for the 1980s.

Gentle and genial, with a neat line in pleasant patter and clever tricks, John Wade had to find his *niche* in this new world. To some extent, he was working against the grain of the inward-looking, somewhat selfish group psychology of the day, for his whole approach was geared – and had been formed by – the communal affinities and collective ethics of the 1940s and 1950s. The climate was now sharper and more individualistic, with many people exhibiting an awful knowingness. It was not strictly a magicianly *ambience*.

John Wade found his career diverting in two directions in the 1980s. Although, at first sight, they appeared different, there was material common ground. Essentially John was a communicator, something that has been quite clear from his schooldays and which, professionally, had also been affirmed by his consistent use as a compere and master of ceremonies. Now, in a new era, that aspect revealed momentum. 'Only connect' was the humane epigraph of E M Forster's 1910 novel, *Howard's End*, and, above all, John Wade personified that wish, blessed, as he was, with the gift and the desire to be a human transmitter. In the first place, John Wade increasingly became a public speaker, usually an after-lunch or post-dinner orator. In the second place, he was in expanding demand as a consultant, especially where some theatrical piece required magical effects.

The speech, of course, included tricks, but the balance of talk to tricks altered substantively. The tricks illustrated the talk, rather than the patter being used to misdirect the watchers. The talk was about the history and development of magic. In the latter case, that of consultation, John Wade was advising producers and designers and tutoring actors about magical efficacy. It might be said that he had taken on a teaching role, informing a lay public about and advising a professional cadre on the magical arts.

In these ways did John come to confront the 1980s. Needless to say, he did not self-consciously select these vocational routeways, any more than Les Dawson positioned himself cognisantly as the herald of the 1980s. That is why the brief Les Dawson profile is germane. Like Les Dawson, John Wade imperceptibly adapted his craft to the novel calls of the age. It was a matter of a series of narrowly specific responses to telephone calls about bookings, not some von Moltke-like master-plan. John Wade would not have altogether realised at those moments that he was refitting himself to new circumstances, nor perhaps did he spot that others, with less flexibility, were fading away. It is only with the slow camera replays of hindsight that one is able to judge where artists and their times conjoin.

From the late 1970s John Wade had received some bookings from the agent, Anthony 'Dabber' Davis. He managed the public speaking agency, Associated Speakers, which was owned by Cyril Fletcher, of 'odd ode' fame. The previous story of public speaking as a commercial enterprise had usually involved an individual lecture or lecture tour. Charles Dickens' readings of his own works, with the murder of Nancy in *Oliver Twist* a particularly exhausting favourite for audience and orator alike, is an example. Nor were such enterprises free of agents. Charles Dickens had been heavily reliant, until his death much mourned by the author, on the business acumen and composure of Arthur Smith. Richard D'Oyly Carte organised Oscar Wilde's lecture tours and, typically, was astute enough to deploy him in the United States just in front of his own touring company of Gilbert and Sullivan's comic opera, *Patience,* with its skit on aestheticism. Oscar Wilde was, in Max Beerbohm's phrase, 'a sandwich-board for *Patience*'. However, the speaking circuits of the last quarter of the 20th century had become a much more expansive industry and Associated Speakers was but the biggest of several such agencies. It included in its effulgent catalogue the likes of Michael Parkinson, David Jacobs and David Kossoff, all examples of names familiar from television coverage, while non-entertainers on the books – Harry Wheatcroft, the roses expert is an instance – were also well-known from their televisual exposure.

A factor in the equation was yet another shift in public leisure values. An element in the widespread collapse of collective leisure was the use of the private car, whilst the merging of gender roles, a concomitant of the social liberalism of the 1960s, led to alterations in leisure attitudes. The young couple of the 1980s might drive together to the shopping centre or the DIY store on a Saturday afternoon, whereas, a generation before, he would have jumped on a bus and gone to the match, leaving her indoors to mind the kids. An outcrop of this was a remarkable switch toward the habit of eating out, which was also encouraged by the adoption by almost every pub, beset by harsh drink-drive penalties, of a catering facility. By 1981 the average two-person household was spending £6 a week on this culinary practice, out of a weekly expenditure on food and drink of £25. This amounted to £300 a year, a quarter of the annual food budget, and this increased over the decade to £500 a year and rising. Ten years before and the habit had scarcely registered on the scales of household spending.

Luncheon and dining clubs were a natural progression from this – and luncheon and dining clubs demanded a speaker. Gradually, the proportion of John Wade's work of this kind outweighed the straightforward cabaret, so let us follow him through a typical working day.

Today it is Cheltenham. This means a relatively early start, making sure the lounge suit is pressed and clean and that the props box, a black square pilot's case, is neat and tidy. John Wade leaves home at 9.30, thus allowing for 'puncture time', and heading for an 11.45 arrival. The venue is the smartest hotel in that leafy market town and John Wade arrives in good time so that he may examine the room, in this instant the main banqueting suite. Sometimes he has the furniture rearranged. He does not want people behind him, not so much because they might see how the tricks are done, more because they might not see anything at all. As a lunch guest, there is not much chance of setting up a table-full of illusions. He finds a point by his place where he can easily utilise his box both for taking out tricks to do and dumping tricks done.

It is a ladies' luncheon club. But few a generation ago, these clubs had sprung up in large numbers over the last two decades and they were a step-change from the Women's Institute and the Townswomen's Guild. They are purely social, meeting for lunch once a month and paying an annual subscription, so as to attract, with, as in John's case, a £300 or £400 fee, an excellent speaker. They are strongly supported and have to be to back so expensive a venture. Lunch is served to between 70 and 200 women, a set menu along the lines of prawn cocktail, chicken and trifle, but arranged with some care by the hotel, for regular bookings in such numbers is a sound staple for its catering business.

Cheltenham in the 1980s is some distance from Tonypandy in the 1950s. To begin with, it is ten times as populous as was Tonypandy in the 1950s. Cheltenham has pushed to well over 100,000 residents, having grown substantially over the last decades and having attracted prosperous modern businesses to its environs. Tonypandy, of course, was devasted by the collapse of the mining industry. Cheltenham's class composition at the time of John Wade's visit was very different to the old-style Tonypandy, with its overwhelmingly working class component in those post-war years. Nearly two-thirds of Cheltenham's economically active population were, in the 1980s, in the top three of the six conventional social classifications. The national average was just over a half for this 'middle class' grouping, while, curiously, Tonypandy's was the exact reverse of Cheltenham's, with but a third in the higher social classes. At that time Tonypandy's unemployment figures were more than double those of the Gloucestershire market town. Cheltenham was and remains smart, comfortable and flourishing. It is a tribute to John Wade's classless and endearing *persona* that his act was as welcome in the Cheltenham of the 1980s as it was in the Tonypandy of the 1950s, as attractive to the well-heeled, ritzy *QEII* passengers as to physically disabled youngsters in Kenya.

Few of the customers for the luncheon club walk or take a bus, as in the old variety days. These are well-to-do ladies, who usually drive to the hotel. In the 1980s there was still a gender imbalance; men in their seventies travelled, on average, twice the mileage as women in their fifties, but these ladies of Cheltenham exemplify the closing gap. There are hints of a sci-fi future. Waiting to speak to a farmers' group in Cambridgeshire once, John Wade noticed that only two or three were present as the clock moved round to the starting time. Suddenly, the sky was darkened by a buzzing cluster of teeny-weeny helicopters. There were ten of them, each carrying two or three agriculturists to the feast, many of them doubtless complaining, in commemoration of a time-honoured five centuries old tradition, of the impoverished condition of farming. The hotel had a special helipad for them, whereas it no longer finds the need to provide a space for anyone in a haywain, drawn by a big horse called Dobbin.

Even during the 20 or so years of speaking at these luncheon clubs, John Wade has noted a couple of changes. The hats have vanished as completely as John's disappearing mirror – 'you don't expect us to wear hats with these expensive hairdos', explained one bareheaded client. The other, more importantly, is the more youthful age of the diners, so much so that a three o'clock finish has become mandatory to leave them free to drive off and pick up the children from school, contributing thereby to a social practice which now accounts for 20% of the morning and evening rush-hour.

Around noon John Wade is met by the president and her committee ('how does it feel like to be the only man among all these women?') and he takes a careful drink or two, calculating to a nicety his alcohol level for the mid-afternoon return journey. Rather like in Aldous Huxley's *Brave New World*, the committee Alphas shield him from the lesser Gammas during the small talk ('how did you come to be a conjuror? – 'I'm the right size to be sawn in half') and then, after the meal and the parish notices, John Wade finds himself upstanding about 1.45 or 2.0 pm. He cheerfully begins thus; 'I'm going to talk to you for about an hour and a half about the history of magic, and, if your eyes glaze over, I'll do a trick . . . I'll do a trick.' In actuality, the postprandial oration, preferably delivered without the inconvenience of a microphone, is normatively of 30 minutes duration and, on occasion, the eyes do glaze over. At one luncheon an elderly lady, located right in front of John because she was hard of hearing, had fallen, numbed by three sweet sherries, into a heavy slumber before he had finished his opening sentence. Part-way through the address, a merry laugh roused her abruptly. She opened and rummaged in a voluminous handbag; drew out a watch; scrutinised it critically; returned it to the bag; struggled to her feet and tottered off into the unknown.

John Wade follows what he calls his stepping stones. Having done his thimbles routine by way of lively introduction, he explains how magic has always been used for entertainment, citing the frame in the ancient pyramid that portrays the magician keeping the building labourers happy, in a kind of preview of *Workers' Playtime*. In the royal courts or out on the streets and in the work-places, that was where magicians plied their craft, asserts John Wade, throwing in his chameleon-like coloured handkerchiefs for good measure. He speaks of Isaac Fawkes, as featured in a Hogarth print, and his magic booth at St Bartholomew's Fair in 18th century London, and he describes how illusions are embellished in rumour and false report, quoting in evidence the Indian rope-trick. According to the tale, the boy climbs the rope, the magician slashes with his scimitar and legs and arms tumble, only for the fully restored boy to be discovered in a nearby bag. In pre-war days Bertram Mills, of big top fame, offered £1000 and the use of the sacrosanct turf of Lord's cricket ground to anyone who could perform the illusion, and his money was safe. At which juncture John Wade performs his invisible pack of cards trick.

On to the story of Robert-Houdin, son of a Blois watchmaker who fled France, a political refugee, at the time of the 1848 liberal revolution. Robert-Houdin hired a London salon and, from 1860, used the St James' theatre for magical shows. His watchmaker's mechanics made him an expert creator of automata and other illusions and he rejoices in the title of 'the Grandfather of Magic'. His main significance lies in his taking magic off the streets and giving it a theatrical setting. An interesting side-effect was that, rather than opt for stagy costumes, he wore the same clothes as his well-heeled audience – and that is why many conjurors still wear white tie and tails. John Wade demonstrates his red and blue boxes, the ones where the larger somehow manages to disappear inside the smaller, before relating how a Jewish American, name of Erich Weiss, working on a fairground, read a book by Robert-Houdin and was inspired not only to devote his life to escapatological illusions but to add an 'i' to the second part of his French Mentor's name and adopt it as his own stage-name.

Pausing only to bend and unbend his famous mirror wrapped in newspaper, John Wade ends with tales of modern illusionists, such as Paul Daniels and David Copperfield, exhibits his *Avengers* card-fans and sits down to a storm of applause. If the storm is tempestuous enough, he rise again and produces, by way of encore, a thin tube, from which he causes to appear a bunch of flowers for presentation to a gratified president. Sometimes there are questions, many of them shrewd, for this is a bright, well-informed gathering, although, at one luncheon, a lady in clerical garb confused John with a query about the 'profits'. When he struggled to speak about monetary gains and losses in the magical trade, she revealed that she had in mind Jeremiah, Ezekiel, Amos, Malachi and their colleagues, wondering whether they had employed magicianly devices.

Now it is close to three o'clock and the primary school gates will be opening. There is an appreciative vote of thanks; there is some discreet sleight of hand which involves an envelope containing a cheque finding its way into John's inside pocket, and soon he is on his way, back home to Bedford Park, maybe a two-hour journey, so that he is preparing a reviving cuppa or tincture by 5.0 or 5.30 pm. It sounds simple enough, slipping out to speak briefly at a lunch, but it has been an eight hour day. Yet not everyone is able to affirm, at the end of an eight hour day, that he has made 200 women happy.

Avenging Pack . . . John Wade exhibits one of the card displays he made famous in the credits of *The Avengers*

It was a mark of his prowess in this field that John Wade was asked by publishers, Hodder and Stoughton, to write a book in their well-known 'Teach Yourself' series, with the title of *Teach Yourself Public Speaking*. John felt he was too busy to undertake the full weight of this, so he recruited the help of Dennis Castle, an expert on the entertainments industry and already the author of three books on public speaking. He provided most of the text, while John provided most of the marketing. It was published in 1980 and sold very well for ten years. In 1984 John Wade was commissioned by Batsford to produce another book on the same theme. *It's Your turn to Speak* also sold quite well and went to a reprint.

In the same context and in the same year, John Wade, that consummate *compère*, also published his guide to that skill, *Do get the name right*, a booklet heartily recommended by, among others, Bob Monkhouse. The man who introduced Gerry Dorsey on one show and then three months later reintroduced him as Engelbert Humperdink has much good sense to impart to budding comperes, including a valued 'Cliché Corner'. But what seems most characteristic of the King's Scout from St Lawrence's C of E Church, Eastcote is the list of artefacts carried in his tiny props case, every item having been found to be of use: 'aspirins, safety pins, a couple of those impregnated tissues they give you on airlines to clean up with, a razor blade, Band-Aids, a nail-file, spare cuff-links and bow tie.' Baden Powell, rest easy.

There was continued media exposure. In 1980 Border Television broadcast *The Magic World of John Wade*, a series of six 15-minute programmes on facets of magic, such as its history, card-tricks, mind-reading and so on. This was the first time John's name had been incorporated into the title of a TV show. Furthermore, as an aspect of the public speaking process, John Wade enjoyed the same titular prominence in Bognor Regis, Tunbridge Wells, Newark, Ruislip and points widespread, with *An Evening with John Wade*, where the format was two 45-minute slots either side of an interval, with questions and other discussion. John had, by now, a reasonable collection of magical memorabilia, including original posters of the old-time celebrity wizards, to augment such events. There was also the comparative luxury of an appearance on Derek Batey's television programme, *Look Who's Talking*, a half-hour of self-indulgent personal reminiscence and opinion and an excellent showcase for John Wade, the public speaker.

For the most part, it was disarmingly pleasant. One was greeted as a rounded person, not as a two-dimensional part of a stage show, and that degree of human recognition mattered considerably to John Wade. He did not wish to be measured merely as a stage magician and what might be called, without undue prissiness, the adult education element of public speaking fortified this resolve. One was well-lunched or dined and there was a general expectation that the fellow-diners were eager to enjoy the occasion. It was a career move that took him to unexpected places, to, for example, London's Guildhall and Mansion House. Not the least of the advantages was that it was well-paid. Many of the engagements attracted a fee of £400 or £500 and there were a couple of memorable occasions, including one in Belfast, when the remittance topped the £1000 mark.

It meant, in turn, that John Wade could pace himself more competently. It meant that he only need do a show a week to maintain a standard of living akin to the upper tiers of professional and managerial existence. It should be remembered that, such was his arthritic ailment, he usually had to enlist the aid of a friend to accompany him on these jaunts, so that he might have a roadie to handle his equipment, even were it only his smaller case of tricks. John was forced to find a balance between what was temptingly offered and what could be sensibly managed. 'Dabber' Davis proved to be what some veteran 'pros' might have regarded as oxymoronic. He was a sensitive theatrical agent, always ready, for instance, to join John on critical or testing occasions.

These bookings through 'Dabber' Davis encompassed that other rising feature of the show-business scene, namely, entertainment at awards banquets and other types of corporate occasion. These were a different kettle of fish to, say, the middle class ladies' luncheon clubs. Indeed, one might urge that they were more typical of the inclement 1980s. The combine of up to 600 young executives with the provision of unlimited alcoholic beverages did not make for a decorous atmosphere. Frenetically intoxicated, egocentrically immature, shallow in human attitude and maniacally selfish, such were their furiously ill manners that security guards had to be employed at some of these high-class functions, not to protect the guests from outside molestation, but from one another and from themselves.

So noisy and inattentive a climate was hardly suited to the amicable dispatch of a few tricks and a couple of easygoing one-liners, but John Wade, although never a combative artist, was forearmed now with thirty-odd years experience. He was well able to cope, equipping himself with a set of what he called 'heckler-stoppers', smart puts-down of the more belligerent clients. He observed how some hard-nosed entertainers, Bob Monkhouse and Jonathan Ross among them, seemed to thrive on this kind of show-business warfare. Like the braver of the Great War soldiery, they could not wait to fix mental bayonets, go over the top, engage with the enemy, preferably in hand-to-hand combat, and return triumphant, having taken no prisoners. It was a skill that an older generation of politicians – one thinks of Lord Hailsham or Harold Wilson – cultivated, to the juncture where they goaded hecklers into committing themselves in order to generate the crosstalk. Sadly, perhaps, today's politicos are safeguarded from such piercing attention by the concentration on the television hustings and the worship of the insidious sound-bite.

Another way in which such warlike comedians had taken a leaf from the shrewd book of politicians like Harold Wilson was by dint of diligence of homework. John Wade found that they were inordinately well-briefed, able to launch verbal attacks of a personal nature on many members of each corporate assembly. On one occasion, after Bob Monkhouse had machine-gunned his lethal fire across such a dining group, John remarked to him, 'you missed one out', such had been the comprehensiveness of his prior study and consequent withering delivery. The nearest approach to this for an older generation would have been the company visit to the local pantomime. An outstanding example might be Metropolitan-Vickers in the 1930s, 1940s and 1950s. An engineering firm, with a huge work-force, at peak, of some 24,000, and based in Trafford Park, Stretford, the company booked the entire house of the Manchester Palace panto for a full week, matinees included. In the days before 'Metros' Week', the panto stars visited the works and took soundings. Come the performances, and they had fingered the pompous managers, the gauleiter foremen, the bolshy trade unionists, the stingy rate-fixers, the operatives who were workshy, over-amorous or otherwise notable, even to the surly canteen waitress – and all would be revealed, through the medium of *Jack and the Beanstalk* or *Babes in the Wood*, to delighted crowds. Maybe there are some continuities.

The other new line was that of consultancy. John Wade was a proficient and inventive magician of some stature, but a consultant has to have not only due expertise, but the skill of conveying that knowledge. Again it was the communicative competence that made the difference: John was a talker, one able to talk agreeably and lucidly about his enthusiasm. A common fallacy about education is that a teacher's first requirement is information, whereas, in truth, at least as important is the ability to develop a working relation with students and motivate them vigorously. The abiding vice of the education system, as John Wade's own experience reminds, is boredom. That is presumably the reason why, even after almost a century and a half of endeavour, the education regime remains, apart from custodial sentences and some mental health orders, the only service reliant for its patronage on legislative compulsion, and, even with that state *diktat*, truancy is rife. When the Billy Cotton band-show played Jersey or Les Dawson played Mistress Trot in panto, there was no need for compulsory attendance regulations; if it is attractive enough, the customers will roll up. There is a creaking and rather prim little tale of a schoolmaster asked by a visiting inspector 'what do you teach?' who responded 'children', but it makes the point and underpins the virtue of John Wade as both speaker and theatrical adviser.

Beginning with a Chichester Festival staging, starring Claire Bloom, in the late 1970s, and including a masterly Lindsay Anderson production, with Dorothy Tutin, at the Haymarket Theatre, London, in 1983, John Wade has tutored five governesses in five runs of Anton Checkov's last play, *The Cherry Orchard*. The playwright's mistress was an actress, but also an amateur conjuror, and he determined to write some magic into the role she played, that of Charlotta Ivanovna, a German governess to the Ranyevskaia family. Near the beginning of Act Three, she does a card trick, finding a chosen card in Simeonov-Pishchik's breast pocket, and then makes the entire pack of cards vanish. Shortly afterwards, she produces her pupil, Ania, from a rug. The playwright caused the illusions to have dramatic significance and to accentuate the flighty, somewhat manic character of Charlotta, and thus thoughtful directors will take a little trouble over the problem. John's most adept student was probably Angela Pleasence, who proved to be a skilful conjuror. Perhaps it was John's tuition that helped lead to her nomination as best supporting actress in the *Evening Standard* annual stage awards.

John Wade has enabled the umbrella – the actress again was Angela Pleasence – to catch fire in Samuel Beckett's *Happy Days*; he taught Ben Cross conjuring for his television portrayal of Charles Dickens, another famed amateur magician; and, along with Alan Shaxon, he schooled Tom Cruise, who, very independent mindedly, refused a stand-in when he had to pass a CD from hand to hand and make it vanish in the 1996 film, *Mission: Impossible.* When Willis Hall and Keith Waterhouse decided to convert J B Priestley's novel of variety theatre, *Lost Empires*, into a musical, with music by Dennis King, it was John who was enlisted for the illusions. J B Priestley was a friend of David Devant and he was fascinated by the world of illusions. He built his story-line around a hard-bitten, cynical illusionist, based on the real-life magician, Claude Singalee. To John Wade's initial horror, the stage designer opted for a revolving stage, thereby denying John the comforts and conveniences of trap-doors. There were benefits. He contrived an effect with the actress who doubled as digs landlady and pub barmaid, in which she circled from lodgings to local, pouring tea and then gin from the same kettle. John was even called upon for a play which opened with a stately butler carrying on his master's false teeth on a silver tray. The gentleman had to put the false teeth in, but the actor still had a full complement of the genuine article, so it took a Wadean conjuring trick to put some bite into that opening scene. The play did not become a very famous piece of theatre.

The employment of John Wade, often on a day rate of between £100 and £200, was a tribute to his teaching ability and also to the directors who recognised, as in *The Cherry Orchard,* that dramatists deserve their instructions to be taken seriously. It is not, then, just a matter of any old trick – it is this specific trick. Moreover, with the whole population the nightly viewers of all kinds of effects on cinema and television screens, theatres had to compete with more energy and flair. John Wade's most spectacular involvement of this kind was with the Royal Birmingham Ballet's production of *The Nutcracker*, first staged in 1990 but repeated annually thereafter, and with a video version to boot.

The director was Sir Peter Wright, chief founder of the ballet company, and this was his gift to the City of Birmingham for its foresight in lending support to the idea. It was a huge undertaking, with, very reasonably, a fee for John Wade of about £1000 to match. John immediately spotted the main hindrance. Unlike the stage play, timing cannot even be momentarily adjusted for magical trickery; the music and the dance pass remorselessly on, and there is no margin for error. However, there was one considerable bonus. Sir Peter Wright insisted that magical consultant must work closely with, not only himself, but the set and costumes designers. This meant, for instance, that the magical props could be tidily colour coded with costumes and sets, and the budget climbed accordingly.

The character Drosselmeyer, a sinister wizard, was the major protagonist of the illusions. He opened his cloak with a bright flash, not the simplest of moves for a dancer; he produced lighted candles of a similar type to those on the Christmas Tree; the silver baubles on the tree floated towards him and back to the tree; he produced coloured streamers from the children's handkerchiefs; a mouse flew up a white cloth and disappeared; the naughty boy decapitated a doll, only for Drosselmeyer magically to replace the head (a radio-controlled illusion that, said a rueful Sir Peter Wright, cost as much as a dancer); with the wizard presumably off-stage, a seemingly empty chair revolved and there he was. The illusions grew ever more sensational. The tree grew so that the candles were the size of humans; the fireplace expanded, and out of the fire raced the now human-sized mice, ready for war; suddenly the toy soldiers had also grown and, taking on humanoid proportions, were ready for hostilities. John Wade deservedly received personal mentions in critical dispatches for his brilliant endeavours.

A conjuring consultancy raises some awkward ethical questions, for the unwritten law of magicians is silence on the business of how tricks are accomplished. John Wade would make two submissions for the defence. First, the magician, like other professionals, also has the duty of bequest, of ensuring that the craft is nourished and passed down to the next generation. John has taught actors discreetly and some of them have remained in touch with him, seeking his advice on other parts with other magical posers. Second, if the play or ballet or film demands magic, magic is, willy-nilly, going to be provided. Far better, then, to guarantee that the effects are achieved to the highest standards than that a mess, practically or artistically, is made of the venture.

And, if Windsor Castle was the accolade of the 1970s *apropos* John's career, another citadel was to fall to his magical charms in the 1980s. The Magic Castle, Hollywood, is the headquarters of American illusionism. It is a membership club for working magicians and a dining club for the laity, and it has three performing areas, a dining room, where close-up magic is the attraction, a parlour for about seventy guests, and a little theatre. In 1983 John was invited to lecture there and, quite daringly, he selected 'Radio Magic' for his theme. It is true that he was undoubtedly the world expert on that esoteric subject, but it was a venturesome choice, nonetheless, for a clientele in part composed of his peers. He prepared and printed a booklet, entitled, *Radio Magic; or, 'Hold this card up to the Microphone so that Everyone can see it'* to distribute on the occasion – and he held enthralled a fascinated audience that included Liza Minnelli and Cary Grant. It was thus in the 1980s that John Wade became a conjuror – and an adult educator – of international note It was a wonderful *coup* and John Wade has since retrod his steps to the Magic Castle, Hollywood many times.

On one of those occasions, as he finished his act, he was unexpectedly granted the accolade of Honorary Life Membership of the Academy of Magical Arts and Sciences, Hollywood, USA. Along with his Membership of the Inner Magic Circle with Gold Star, it fittingly represented his wide international recognition.

Chapter Six
THE 1990s
WHAT IS THIS LIFE . . .

Aunt Elsie died and left her nephew, John, a few bob.

One should apologise for introducing his sainted aunt at such an advanced stage of the plot and then only in order to record her sad demise. Those who have cherished the detail of chapter one will recall that an anonymous person, presumably a relative, bought the toy box of conjuring tricks which was, as they used to say of Serajevo and the Great War, 'the spark that lit the powder train.' If romance ruled, it would have been and possibly was Aunt Elsie. Then she would have both stimulated the beginning of John Wade's career and also succoured the close of it.

Elsie Wade, George Wade's sister, was a spinster aunt, but not old maidish. She held down quite a high-powered post in the civil service. Living alone on a reasonable salary allowed her to splash out a little; she travelled abroad and she became interested in art, buying a few paintings for herself as souvenirs of her foreign holidays. She died in 1995. In the aftermath of that exploding powder train of 1914-1918, shrewd women spotted opportunities. Having proved valuable as domestically based workers during the war and won, not least because of that, the right to vote, the sorrowful gaps in manpower gave some women a chance to make their way in the civic professions like medicine, teaching, local government and the civil service, especially if they refrained from marriage. Tales used to be told in school staffrooms of women teachers who pretended they were single and wore their wedding rings around their necks.

Relatively Influential . . . Aunt Elsie

Elsie Wade remained unmarried and she was the only one of the Wade extended family to rise to the comfort of a decent middle class salary and – if her experience matched that of others in her situation – she was probably a tiny bit suspected and resented by the poorer menfolk in the family. In essence, Elsie Wade and her sisterhood were the successors to the ardent suffragette campaigners of the Edwardian era and the predecessors of the feminist wave of the New Elizabethan period. Quieter than the former and primmer than the latter, they nevertheless forged a link in the chain back to that moment in 1867 when John Stuart Mill proposed in the House of Commons that women should have the vote – and historians still cannot decide whether the ribald guffaws that met this suggestion were laughter at him, as an ass, or with him, as a wit. He did, however, secure 73 votes for his amendment, so a start had been made.

What's more, Aunt Elsie left her nephew, John, a few bob.

This was the enjoyable element in a combine of factors that permitted John Wade to relax in the last years of the century and continue his expansion, dating from the 1960s, of becoming a more three-dimensional person. A second one accorded to the pain rather than the pleasure principle. As well as the tautening rack of arthritis, he was subjected to a spinal ailment of alarming proportions. It caused him to lock up suddenly, unable to bend or move, and stricken with appalling agony. Nothing could be done to assist him; it was a matter of waiting patiently for slow release. It was bad enough in the privacy of his sitting room, but it happened a couple of times whilst he was swimming, something which he was encouraged to do as a help for the arthritis. Now that was frightening, with a distinct risk of drowning, and John had to take care he swam, if at all, with a companion close by.

The cartilage between vertebrae two and three had all but worn away, causing fusion of the said bones. After some years of additional discomfort, John Wade underwent an operation in 1998 for the installation of a carbon steel cage around the painful area, in which was sewn a chip of bone from his hip, so that new bone would develop within that metal gaol and vertebrae two and three would behave themselves a little more conventionally. It worked well enough. John grew an inch as his body straightened; the pain wrinkles cleared from his face, and he was no longer reduced to eating his tea off the top of the piano. Nonetheless, what with the arthritis and the stiff back, he had to watch his workload prudently – becoming physically locked in the middle of urging the larger box to enter the smaller box was not conducive to excellence of performance.

A third aspect concerned the nature of magical work in itself. There was a shift toward close-up magic, with conjurors operating on the small scale at individual tables. This was in pursuit of two social indicators. One we have already encountered; it was the widespread delight in eating out. Hotels and restaurants increasingly employed magicians to entertain their customers, whiling away the stray minutes between courses and shuffling their cards amid the culinary debris. The other facet was television. This had introduced and accustomed viewers to close-up magic, with tricks performed at a much shorter range than in the theatre or club. This was a little game with own goals scored, for John Wade himself, from his window cleaning commercials to his *Avengers* credits, had been prominent among those whose hands had become household digits. Moreover, cinema and television could provide large masterly visual effects and perhaps people were growing complacent, even surfeited, by 'Star Wars' technology. Close-up magic, right under the eyeballs of the punter, was in demand and, furthermore, it suited the privatism of the era, the partial retreat from the collective experience of entertainment as of other aspects of existence. One's companion or family and oneself had one's very own magician, if only for five minutes, at one's very own table.

Plainly, John Wade did not take too kindly to this change. This was not because of any technical problem, but because he found it boring. A showman, a child of variety and end-of-pier bookings, he found the perambulation around umpteen tables doing the same set of tricks umpteen times for handfuls of people was tedious in the extreme, at least compared with the buzz of amusing a thousand-strong audience. It is the difference between Tony Hancock, buttonholing individuals on their settees for 30 minutes by the radio or in front of the television set, with his preposterously uncertain valour ('What about Magna Carta? Did that poor Rumanian girl die for nothing?' – 'It is a far, far better thing that I do than I have ever done. Rembrandt') and the four hour destruction by laughter of a great host by Ken Dodd, that evangelist of mass comedy ('What a wonderful day it is to run down the road sticking cucumbers through people's letter boxes and shouting 'the Martians are coming'')

Conjuror's Castle .. John Wade's West London home for 40 years

These three factors, the financial, the physiological and the professional, mixed to make John Wade take things more easily during the 1990s. Like many entertainers, musicians and artists, he had no pension beyond that offered by the state. Self-employed, money had come in fits and starts. He had once opened a pension fund account, but, as Noel Coward sang, 'there are bad times just around the corner', and, when dates dried up, this could not be maintained and was aborted. Aunt Elsie's inheritance was a godsend. John Wade invested it prudently in a building society; promptly lost a thousand pounds and decided instead to spend it on improving his quality of life, with a better than average holiday here and a more sumptuous than usual party there.

However, his main deployment of this money, not least in honour of Aunt Elsie herself, was in the purchase of pictures. John Wade realised, with something of a surprise, that he was interested in art. Ever since his schooldays, when he had enjoyed the vivid paintings of Toulouse-Lautrec to the horror of his staid mother, this had, intermittently, been the case. During his touring days, he had invariably visited the local art gallery, in part because he believed that this is what visitors to a town did. Over the years this built into a considerable amount of experience, so that, with more time and a little money, he was able later to indulge this pastime sensibly and appreciatively.

The Savage Club was again at his elbow. Just as its medical members had ushered him through the arthritic crisis, now the artistic members tutored him about paintings and photographs. The painter, John Seabrook, was dean of this particular faculty. Like Thomas Hardy's Giles Winterbourne in *The Woodlanders,* 'he was one of nature's very gentlemen'. Charmingly affable and gifted withal, he accompanied John to many an exhibition, conversing pleasantly and teaching unobtrusively and without condescension. John Wade has half a dozen Seabrook paintings and charcoal sketches in his collection.

There are *longuers* in show-business. There is a lot of what taxi drivers call waiting time. In theatre dressing rooms, in radio and television studios, on film sets, with free time in strange towns and on lengthy journeys, there is a place for hobbies, such as John Wade's *penchant* for art galleries. Marquetry was another relaxation, as might be expected of he who had carved model aeroplanes in war-time and constructed magical equipment in peace-time. John's dressing room usually included a piece of marquetry – for instance, a side-table, with the four playing card pips inlaid on its veneer – and, when the arthritis threatened, colleagues had to be enlisted to do the vigorous sandpapering that was required. During the Sunderland panto run of *Aladdin* Peter Goodwright earned himself more than one bottle of Guinness for a ten minute bout of rubbing down the wooden bases.

There were crosswords and John Wade and Aunt Elsie have in common, apart from their love of the visual arts, both being winners of the *Times* crossword competition. There was reading, for the advantage of those long train journeys in the 1950s had been the scope it allowed to develop that good habit. Car usage restricted but never halted his affection for reading. By the 1980s and 1990s John Wade gradually edged away from English to American literature of early 20th century vintage. He sought a vital world he could not know, one made alive to him through the pages of Ernest Hemingway, John Steinbeck, John O'Hara, Scott Fitzgerald, J D Sallinger, O'Henry and Sinclair Lewis.

The increased leisure of the 1990s also permitted him to study in more detail the science of magic and research the origins of tricks. In particular, he traced the background to the conjuring exploits of *littérateurs* like Charles Dickens, in his wizardly guise of Rhia Rhama Rhoos, or Lewis Carroll, whose evocation of the vanishing Cheshire Cat is based on Pepper's Ghost, the illusion in which the body disappears, leaving a skull remaining, without the use of a box. For a magic show in the Isle of Wight in 1849 Charles

Dickens proudly announced himself as 'the Unparalleled Necromancer . . . Educated cabbalistically in the Orange Groves of Salamanca and the Ocean Caves of Alum Bay'.

The 1990s also witnessed the furtherment of the communication revolution, with a menu of microchips with everything. Few will be astonished to learn that John Wade, the gadget-king, was a willing disciple of every last turn of the fax, desktop publishing, computerdom and Email machinery. One recalls his patent joy in the arrival from America into his gleeful possession of a James Bond-oriented device, shaped like a silver gherkin, to which one could privily consign messages.

John Wade also found more time in the 1990s to pursue his lifelong love-affair with the metropolis, visiting its galleries, but also walking its streets and admiring its other attractions. Acquainted with its energetic spirit as a boy through the good offices of his father, John strides in the wake of Samuel Johnson and Charles Dickens and of other quintessential lovers of London. For all his widespread travels, both professional and vacational, John's is a metropolitan soul and he is never happier than at the epicentre of the city where he was born and bred and schooled, where he has found the core and bulk of his work as a jobbing conjuror and the best of that which has made of him a rounded social being, and where he has discovered himself as a discrete person.

And the 1990s were not a bad time to relax a little. A more generous spirit was abroad after the abrasive tenor of the 1980s. Not only in the United Kingdom but across much of the developed world, bridges were being built, with Bill Clinton, shrugging off personal flaws, offering a lead with his polished political charisma. There were attempts, admittedly sometimes halting, to reconcile the tensions between private commercial adventure, that sometimes brought distress, and necessary public facilities, that were often ponderous in delivery. A thriving global economy, founded on the wings of electronic communion, promised fuller employment after a lean spell in that regard. The value of the global bond market leapt from $4 trillion dollars in 1980 to $34 trillion dollars in 2000. While social ills remained endemic, with, for example, a third of UK property crimes drugs-related and two-fifths of violent crime and four-fifths of criminal damage alcohol-related, there seemed room for a little more optimism.

This was underlined by the collapse of the Soviet bloc of countries after 1989 and their embrace of western values. Democratic governance, with acceptable public services and strong central regulation as the checks on otherwise liberal capitalist economics appears to be the salient planetary lifestyle. A complex political measure suggests that civil rights and freedoms have grown over the last 30 years. Of the world's 191 nation-states, 43 were graded 'free' in 1970; in 2000 the number had surged to 88, while the 'unfree' figure had dropped from 67 to 50, leaving 53 in 2000, as opposed to 34 in 1970, 'partly free'.

It is an impressive enough record to have caused Francis Fukuyama to argue in his controversial book, *The End of History,* that there is no viable alternative to liberal democracy and that, to all intents and purposes, the political record may be closed. Although he has fiercely urged that these represent the last throes of primitive and outmoded regimes, the catastrophic events in the USA of September 11, 2001 and the subsequent Afghan campaign have made many commentators less sanguine. Nor are the harsh problems of the Middle East and the Sub-continent easily ignored. Nonetheless, John Wade was relatively fortunate in the Hobson's Choice of his seventh decade as a time for running down the engine and enjoying himself a little.

What he did, professionally, was to reap the rewards of 40 years of experience, cherry picking activities that he was eager to do and eschewing those about which he was not so keen. Psychologically, it was a slightly testing experience. John Wade was a man who had lived for 40 years with one ear cocked for the trill of the telephone bell and for whom the word 'no' choked in his throat. Trying to adapt to the strangeness of uttering negatives to people anxious to pay him money, he continued to undertake some speaking and cabaret engagements, while, at the same time, concentrating on a few different and high profile shows.

Among these was a radio programme, *The Music of Magic*, which he struggled hard to have broadcast and which proved extraordinarily successful. This was in August 1990 and was in BBC Radio Two's *Friday Night is Music Night* series. John Wade devised, wrote and presented the show, featuring the BBC Concert Orchestra in songs, excerpts and compositions, such as *Danse Macabre, It's Magic, Ace of Hearts, The Magic Flute* and *The Sorcerer's Apprentice*. It was recorded at the Golders Green Hippodrome. The accompanying illusions included the conductor, Barry Wordsworth, being sawn in half by John Wade and Alan Shaxon with an electric saw, batons, rather than the usual swords, having been thrust through his body, and a thought reading act by which, from a bag full of a hundred song-titles, the one pressed to the forehead of an innocent member of the audience miraculously turned out to be the one – *Always* – which the pianist, Eric Parkin, after much mock internal cogitation, played. The programme was repeated on a larger scale in 1992 at St. David's Hall, Cardiff, with Barry Wordsworth conducting the Welsh Symphony Orchestra. It being April Fools' Day, *It's Magic* was played backwards.

There were two professional visits to Las Vegas. One of them involved acting as compere for a three day convention in the Riviéra Hotel, Buggsy Malone's own. This was organised by the Society of American Magicians in 1991. Realising that one of the days coincided with Independence Day, John Wade proffered the audience a tea-bag and asked whether we could have our colonies back. Another highlight was in 1993 when John Wade arranged an exhibition at the Museum of the Moving Image on London's South

Bank. This commemorated the work of the French magician, Meliès, whose activities touched on the early deployment of moving film. His magic shop in Paris was lovingly reproduced for the exhibition, along with his influential illusions, some of them on primitive film.

As part of the 1993 *Children in Need* exercise, John Wade supervised the decapitation of John Humphrys, the feisty BBC political interviewer. The Ko Ko role was taken by cabinet minister John MacGregor, himself an amateur conjuror, with, as his assistants, two other MPs, Simon Hughes and Teresa Gorman, representative of the many politicians who might fervently have wished for their scourge to be silenced, if not quite so drastically as with a beheading. John continues to engage in charitable endeavour, with, for example, Stage for Age, the theatrical fund-raising group backing the charity Help the Aged.

Riper years give pause for retrospect. The ceaseless journeyings about the globe of a magician of international status lend a particular and immediate resonance to such recollections. The memories are little and large. For example, John Wade joyfully recalls the fairly recent delight of browsing in a bookshop in the small town of Longview, Texas and finding not one but two copies of his *Teach Yourself Magic Tricks* book. He bought one – and another customer, attracted by the ecstatic cries of a proud author, bought the other and claimed an autograph. But there are the more panoramic memories. Blanche and John met in a South Africa riven by the evil of Apartheid, scarcely daring to hope that one day they would see Nelson Mandela walk free from prison in 1990 and preside over a freer and more democratic South Africa. They scuttled through Checkpoint Charlie, penetrating through the grim grey Berlin Wall, hardly allowing themselves the wish that it would tumble and that Eastern Europe, too, would reach out for liberty. Remembrance is not all delectable. On his many *QEII* trips John Wade gazed on and admired the erection of the twin towers of

New York's World Trade Centre, never imagining that, in September 2001, he would stare horror-stricken at their fiery destruction.

John Wade was also now able to find more time to devote to the Savage Club, of which he has been a member for 40 years. He was chairman of the Club from 1991 to 1993 and remains prominent within its senior counsels. Historians wrangle over whether the human condition is normatively one of peace with intermittent war, or *vice versa.* Observers of the Savage Club's internal economy similarly ponder whether its norm is the wolf pressing at the door, with occasional retreats to the comparative relief of the garden gate, or the other way around. That lupine creature was assuredly clawing at the portals during John's incumbency. As Ken Barrington, the former England cricketer and manager, once said of an English Test team in India, 'we were clinging on by our eyelashes.' The Savage Club had recently been obliged to make an expensive move and was teetering on the precipitous brink of sheer survival.

John's skills were invaluable, as in his procuring a full-page article on the club in the *London Evening Standard*, and in other public relations ways, while others, more fiscally adjusted, sweated over the accounts. Above all, John Wade, characteristically, brought hope. That undaunted *esprit,* the optimistic resolution that had conquered the gloomy doubts cast on his youth and fought the troubles and ailments of his middle years, the bright-eyed *panache* that, from Tonypandy in the 1950s to Cheltenham in the 1980s, had spurred on the fizzing attack of his magic act, now came to the aid of the Club which had so succoured and stimulated him. John Wade was the Savage Club's standard bearer. Another crisis was averted; the Savage Club survives; the wolf, for the moment, prowls the path midway between the door and the garden gate.

John Wade spends time at the Savage Club – and he also spends time on it, principally in his role as the club's 'Watchman', a kind of almoner post, whereby he endeavours to keep open an eye for those members or the families of past members who may have fallen into some slough of distress, financial or social. This task he fulfils with zeal, yet never with an overbearing patronage. Sensitive and, as one would expect, very practical, he operates his watchmanship on behalf of the club's charitable benevolent fund with manifest compassion. *The Screwtape Letters* inform us that you can always tell who is being done good to from the hunted look in their eyes. John Wade studiously finds the sympathetic balance between assistance and interference and the eyes are invariably appreciative.

In microcosm, his Watchman's post at the Savage Club may serve as a key to John Wade's basic attitude to life and its living. Like many entertainers who have had to make their way in a chilly world, clambering out on to the stage alone, perhaps with a throat – one recalls John's first panto at Chester – clogged and hoarse, to try and woo a sometimes sullen audience, there is much of the individualist about him. The struggle to find a place in the show-business arena is a tough one and John Wade is keenly conscious of the fact that, in the last analysis, you are on your own. It is one's own responsibility to seize and make the chances. It is not about a lack of trust in others to give support; far from it, and John is first in the queue when it comes to heaping praise on those who, in both his personal and professional life, have befriended and boosted him. It is more a recognition that, eventually, the onus lies on one's own personality.

At the same time, again like many other entertainers, there is an instinctive generosity to give and to assist in charitable ventures and so on. In John's case this is underlaid by a genuine concern that, while chances must be grasped, everyone deserves a chance. Opportunity may only knock once, but it should knock for everybody. If one were, without undue ostentation, to develop that duality of respect for self and concern for others into something resembling a philosophic tenet, then one might do worse than raid the intellect of another John, viz, Stuart Mill of that ilk.

John Stuart Mill's Victorian social liberalism invoked a society in which compromise was sought between freedom in everything that concerned the individual and discipline in everything that concerned the community. It is messy and ambivalent, for, in the borderlands between the two, there is constant friction about what falls where. At best, however, it can be a creative tension. It does urge an acceptance that both the personal and the collective have their place and that all relevant judgements necessitate apt joint consideration. John Wade, like many of his generation, has lived through years in which politicians and nations have concentrated on the one extreme or the other, denying the alternative wholesale or granting it but grudging recognition. A social *credo* that encompasses both pushing yourself and pulling for others remains, for John Wade, whatever the pedantic objections, a sane rule of thumb for the conduct of life.

John Wade crowned the Millennium with his 70th birthday. Accidents and designs have conspired to make him the very model of a modern senior citizen. It has been estimated that, if all the odd minutes and hours are totted up when people are not working or involved in other duties, such as child-rearing or housework, then the average European adult has 3000 notional days of leisure before retirement and 8000 days afterwards. Put another way, the average British life ending in 1900 would have enjoyed 40,000 hours of leisure, whilst the average life concluding in 2000 would have been indulged to the tune of 250,000 hours of leisure potential, much of it in later life.

Alarmingly, the British take retirement very seriously. They retire with a vengeance. They withdraw into the anterooms of society and, with twice as much leisure opportunity as the employed adult, the retired adult does little constructive in that direction. In the indices of recreational activity, from going to the cinema to gardening or just taking a walk, there is only one indicator where older people are more prolific than younger people. That is watching television. People over 60 currently watch, on average, 39 hours a week, compared with 26 hours for the population at large. Immediately a gaggle of protests is heard in the land from pensioners proclaiming that they pack so much into their retired existences that they do not know how they once managed to fit in going to work. They are the ones at the front, shouting, the ones we hear. Behind them are phalanx after phalanx of the silent majority of Doctor Dolittles.

There are some material explanations in regard of ill-health and inadequacy of income, but the cultural explanations are also very revealing. The perceptive community physician, John Muir Gray, has developed the clinical thesis of 'the Fitness gap', the gulf that grows with age between what you can do and what you do do. He has demonstrated that, in good measure, one reason for this is that older people believe the thousand-year propaganda campaign about the association of ageing with decrepitude and willingly play out the role in which they have been cast. Without the construct of work to schedule and identify their lives, many have the social rug pulled from under them. The imagery is vivid. What was once 'a slip of memory' easily becomes 'my memory's going'. Old women advertise soup and brown bread, but never deodorant or showergel. Older people are not only the victims; they are part of the conspiracy.

Probably to his utter and shattering astonishment, John Wade has avoided these pitfalls and bids fair to becoming the archetype for older age in the 21st century, and may he long be maintained in that exemplar role. One of the curses of the entertainments industry has been that its workers have been often compelled to toil on, possibly beyond the sell-by date of act and body, for stark economic reasons. One of its benefits is that, if you are able and if you are still in demand, it is possible to continue without such compulsion. John Wade, with a tad of help from Aunt Elsie, hasn't so little money that he has to labour on, but he is not so well funded that it makes good sense to stop, especially when the telephone continues to ring. It is true that he has suffered ill-health, but that is not especially age-related and, over more than 30 years, he has grittily come to terms with it.

Like Karl Marx's dream that urban and rural circumstances would blend into a worldly paradise, John Wade's work and leisure have imperceptibly merged into a seamless whole that has not suffered the fell Guillotine of officious retirement. What is more, it is a life that is outgoing, positive and giving, as well as balanced as among its technical, artistic, social and other features. The morning in the art gallery; the session at the Savage Club; the visit to a fellow-member sick in hospital; the speaking engagement at a function out in Hertfordshire; the evening spent in research, perhaps into one of the magicians – the legendary David Devant; Charles Bertram, who did card tricks for the Prince of Wales, afterwards King Edward VII; Lionel King, who could force a card on you with the pack behind his back – who form, with John Wade, a magical lineage in the Savage Club's saga; the profoundly recuperative yet inspiriting week in Germany with Blanche . . .

Inquiring, restlessly curious, thrilled with the latest electronic apparatus, hesitating over the next Guinness or glass of whisky then deciding to take the plunge, beaming rays of *bonhomie* to all his myriad friends . . . such is John Wade. With good management of his good luck, he has knocked together – it would be too fictitious to declare it was purposefully constructed – a rough and ready life that, in its essential character, has not changed a jot from when he mixed mending fuses, singing tremulously in the church choir, chivvying his boy scout patrol, making model aeroplanes and embarking on exotic bike rides into the Middlesex and Buckinghamshire countryside with the teenage belles of Pinner, as a cheery school-lad well over half a century ago.

The comic creation of Mr Pickwick by the young Charles Dickens envisioned a picaresque novel of the *Tom Jones* brand, but with the itinerant hero having the heart and nerve of the erstwhile youngster locked in the crumbling physique of an older man. It makes for a delectable confection, but a century and a half of affectionate attachment suggests it is a humane conceit that evinces our proper admiration. John Wade, sea-dog's pipe, greying hair, arthritic limbs and dodgy back notwithstanding, somehow preserves that innate gladsomeness of youth. Thus, as Richmal Crompton once ended a story about William:

> *We will leave him as, pale and unsteady, but as yet master of the situation, he wends his homeward way.*

Oh yes he did . . . John now having achieved some of his ambitions and still working on others

AFTERWORD
REFLECTIONS IN A MAGIC MIRROR

John Wade writes:

Eric suggested that I should contribute some pages of my own, and I shall endeavour to set down a few disjointed thoughts in the hope that, if you have read this far, they might have some small value. So with a Macallan to hand and the pipe puffing away satisfactorily, here goes.

Noel Coward managed to sum up my life in a couple of lines, although, of course, our paths never crossed – would that they had. He wrote in a song:

> *I believe that since my life began,*
> *The most I've had is just*
> *A talent to amuse . . .*

I have been incredibly lucky in the places I have been able to visit and the people I have met along the way. In over 50 years of doing magic tricks and hopefully amusing people with what has always seemed to me a slender talent, it would be surprising if I had not had a few adventures worth recounting. When laughter is around and the stories are flowing, it is then that the siren words are uttered: 'you should write all these stories down and publish a book.' But the idea of writing yet another show business autobiography never appealed. There are so many of what I call 'First I went to school and then I did and then I met . . .' type of books about, and like these books, and a few I have had published over the years, the unautographed copies are often the rarest. Larry Adler wanted to call his own autobiography *Name-drops keep falling from my head,* but he could and did drop real names.

It was only after conversations with several academics that it dawned on me how much change had been going on behind my working life, from variety theatres closing, through television, cabaret, radio, cruising, night clubs and public speaking, that I realised that to set the stepping stones of this jobbing conjuror against the huge social changes taking place might be of interest. When my friend the Social Historian showed how such a story might be told, it seemed to good an opportunity to miss, and thus it was that Eric Midwinter and I started on our series of interviews.

To try to cast one's mind back to one's childhood and recall the trivia of the daily round of going to school or church during the blitz was very hard for me, and yet, unbidden, a smell or taste can bring the whole period back with total clarity. Answering Eric's questions was stimulating and yet very tiring. Three hours was about all I could manage without losing concentration. Then on the tube home afterwards a stack of material would come to mind which, with luck, I might remember to bring to the next session.

It cannot be easy for anybody under 50 to understand how much the word 'war' meant to my generation. My dad experienced two world wars. Like most of those who went through the first one, he said very little about it. His permanent cough he put down to what he called a 'whiff of gas', and the dreadful London fog of 1952 probably finished off the job that the Kaiser had started. In the second war, when he came back to London, he was put on Firewatcher duties on the Air Ministry roof, and I recall him coming home one morning, just as I was about to leave for school, his face covered in soot and grime, as he had been in the Holborn Empire trying to extinguish the fires resulting from the night's bombing. Many years before he had seen Little Tich there, a comedian now only recalled in a flickering black and white minute or two on TV from time to time, but, to my dad, the funniest man he had ever seen.

Dad could add up rows of figures in his head and first introduced me to some of the number puzzles I later did on radio. How he would have enjoyed pocket calculators, but, sadly, he died before they came out. He did not see colour television, and would have enjoyed digital watches, tape recorders and videos. He would have enjoyed my computer-oriented son's bewildering array of electronic apparatus and probably have been just as mystified by it as I am.

When I came out of the Royal Air Force, it was dad who suggested that we met in London at the Air Ministry one morning. As we walked, he told me that under my feet was a honeycomb of tunnels, some only a foot or two below me, others very deep indeed. This, and his knowledge of London churches, many, sadly, only bombed out shells by then, must have kindled my interest in what has become 'my city.' He would have enjoyed the fact that I became a Freeman of the City of London about 50 years after he had first told me that it was possible to do so.

Although I consider myself to be a Londoner, my trade has taken me around so much that I have probably seen more of my country than many others. I have walked Hadrian's Wall, explored the Lake District, trod the field of Culloden and enjoyed every bit of it. Three times have I stayed in the wonderful Gleneagles Hotel and never ever seen it in daylight, flying up in the late afternoon to do whatever function it was, and then getting up before daybreak to catch the first plane home. But home to London is where I always happily return, feeling at once secure in that overcrowded, polluted city, among the red buses, black taxicabs and the vagaries of the District Line.

One constant thing I have noticed in my life as a single stand-up performer is the aloneness of the life. Not loneliness, for I have been lucky seldom to have experienced that, but the fact that for so much time I have been alone. So often I have left an applauding audience, high on the adrenaline, to get into my car and drive 200 miles or so through sleeping villages and nearly empty motorways, with only the radio for company. Looking back, I suppose the car and the radio were the most important components of my working life. In the days when I used to drive about 30,000 miles a year, I became intimately involved with the world of what went on under a car's bonnet. Plugs, points, alternators, brake shoes and wheel changing were as much a part of my working life as the packs of cards I used. Now if I lift the bonnet of my car I am confronted by such an array of technology that I wouldn't know a gasket from a fuel injector, and I try never even to look there. I used to keep a container of grease remover as part of my general kit, after arriving at a posh venue to be my well-dressed and suave performing self but first having to remove a thick layer of black grease from my finger nails.

I have always preferred radio to television, both to work on and listen to. The first time I crossed the imposing threshold of the BBC in Portland Place to take apart in a real live broadcast was one of the high spots of my life. These days I often find myself in my tiny office being interviewed for radio on my own telephone, trying to keep the cat from walking across the phone and cutting me off while I do it, but it isn't a patch on being in a proper studio being a proper broadcaster.

I headed these few pages with a verse by Noel Coward and I will close by quoting Hilaire Belloc. I find even this a bit odd, since my

English teachers at school so spoilt any poetry or Shakespeare for me that it took many years before I realised Shakespeare wrote his plays to be performed to, and understood by, a wide popular audience, and that the same applied to the best of poetry. Much too late in life I began to enjoy both. Before I hand you back to my probing and perceptive Boswell (and we are still friends so far) here is what Belloc wrote:

From quiet homes and first beginning,
Out to the undiscovered ends,
There's nothing worth the wear of winning,
But laughter and the love of friends.

Under no illusion . . . John Wade chairs a Savage dinner, with Paul Daniels as the guest of honour

Eric Midwinter writes:

This has been a genuinely earnest attempt at biography, although the circumstances have been a little unusual. John Wade had been considering some memoir of his intriguing career. For my part, a recent stint of preparing notices of the lives of a baker's dozen of comedians for *The New Dictionary of National Biography* had re-opened a seam of research untouched for some time. I was thinking about a piece of writing on the social background of entertainment in the post-war period. John had been anxious, in his planned reminiscences, to comment on how his career had been both aided and hindered by alterations on the broader social canvas over 50 years in the show-business trade, and this, obviously, suited my wish to do something from the stance of social history.

A couple of lunchtime discussions later we had embarked on this collaboration. We determined on a kind of 'bio-documentary.' John Wade's personal story would be logged, but in the changing context of society in general and its leisure industry in particular. The methodology has been straightforward. We have had umpteen question and answer sessions in the Savage Club, followed by speedily done drafts, rapidly composed while memory was fresh and before hopes had dimmed of deciphering my own notes. Occasional printed and written evidence was introduced, as it suggests in *The Mikado,* 'to give artistic verisimilitude to an otherwise bald and unconvincing narrative.'

Biographies range from the hagiographic to the muck-raking. This life-story possibly falls in between these two extremes. It is, after all, the product of many conversations between two good friends. We have attempted to offer an accurate account, the conjuror in respect of recall of information, the biographer in regard of arbitration about the significance of the data, but it would be folly to pretend that it is a disinterested narrative. That said, there are still advantages in the biographical over the autobiographical technique.

At its simplest, it is difficult not to sound boastful, in a self-oriented memoir, when relating what might be a quite ordinary achievement: the biographer does not have that worry. He may call the spade that has dug successfully for victory a spade. More importantly, the biographer may notice some aspect of the subject's life from a differing angle. It might be something the individual has taken for granted or assumed that his reaction is the same as everyone else's — and that might just be the facet which the observer spots as being idiosyncratic or otherwise strikingly singular, a trait that illumines the life. Perhaps the most fascinating moments of this present process have been when John Wade has been startled, even embarrassed, by how he is being viewed.

Few narratives are, in reality, free of one bias or another and, of course, this is a friendly account. When we began this project, John Wade said to me very solemnly, 'you don't have to like me', but interestingly, the critical thread in his self-history is that John Wade has always been personally likeable and that – in what proportions spontaneous and conscious it is difficult to gauge – he was and remains professionally likeable. It has been the wellspring of his success, as betokened by the fact that his many engagements as a compere and after-meal speaker arise from that quality as much as from his magical skills.

So it would be astonishing were his storyteller not to share that popular judgement. The picture painted, in these pages is based on that more everyday kind of estimate of John's work and life. It is what you might call a people's verdict, perhaps the portrait almost all his friends would affectionately recognise.

In a flagrant act of plagiarism, I turn, at the end, to that now rather underestimated author, Arnold Bennett. John Wade's career has been much involved with cards, but there is a definite flavour about his life that recalls Arnold Bennett's alternative card. His story, *The Card,* was published in 1911, just as George and Amy Ward were nearing adolescence. It tells of the adventures of Denry Machin in the 'Five Towns' of the Stoke-on-Trent area and is based on the wheeler-dealing activities of Arnold Bennett's ebulliently loveable fellow-townsman, H K Hales. The novel concludes with an account of Corporation Sunday, with Edward Henry Machin (his mum called him Denry to save time) installed as mayor. It may accurately stand as a popular judgement on John Wade.

> *A little group of councillors were discussing Denry. What a card!, said one, laughing joyously. He's a rare 'un, no mistake.*
> *Of course, this'll make him more popular than ever,' said another. We've never had a man to touch him for that.*
> *And yet, demanded Councillor Barlow, what's he done? Has he ever done a day's work in his life? What great cause is he identified with?*
> *He's identified, said the speaker, with the great cause of cheering us all up.*

Index

Other books by Eric Midwinter for Third Age Press

... is a series that focuses on the presentation of your unique life. These booklets seek to stimulate and guide your thoughts and words in what is acknowledged to be not only a process of value to future generations but also a personally beneficial exercise.

A Voyage of Rediscovery: a guide to writing your life story
A Voyage of Rediscovery is a 'sea chart' to guide your reminiscence. It offers 'triggers' to set your memory to full steam ahead (although backwards might be more appropriate) & provides practical advice about the business of writing or recording your story.
NEW edition 2001 36pages ISBN 1 898576 00 9 £4.50

Encore: a guide to planning a celebration of your life
An unusual and useful booklet that encourages you to think about the ways you would like to be remembered, hopefully in the distant future. **20 pp ISBN 1 898576 02 5 £2.00**

The Rhubarb People . . . Eric Midwinter's own witty and poignant story of growing up in Manchester in the 1930s. . . is published as a booklet but also as a 90-minute audio cassette read by the author. The cassette includes useful tips on writing or recording your story. **32pages ISBN 1 898576 01 7 £3.00**
~ audio cassette £5.00

OR ~ all three booklets [The Lifelines Pack] for only £7.50

and >>>>>>>>>>>>>